EMPIRICAL
SOCIAL RESEARCH
IN GERMANY
1848-1914

PUBLICATIONS OF THE
INTERNATIONAL SOCIAL SCIENCE COUNCIL

PARIS   MOUTON & CO   THE HAGUE

MCMLXV

ANTHONY OBERSCHALL

EMPIRICAL
SOCIAL RESEARCH
IN GERMANY
1848-1914

PARIS   MOUTON & CO   THE HAGUE
MCMLXV

Published with the assistance of the
BUREAU OF APPLIED SOCIAL RESEARCH
(COLUMBIA UNIVERSITY)
and the
ÉCOLE PRATIQUE DES HAUTES ÉTUDES
(SORBONNE)

Preface

Today the development of contemporary sociology on a variety of fronts is taken for granted. A theoretical discussion of the nature of social systems is part of our field just as is a survey of public opinion or an analysis how physicians can keep up with progress in medicine after they have completed their formal training. The times when religious wars were fought over the relative merits of social theory and empirical research are fortunately past. Those earlier days have been superseded not only by mutual tolerance but by collaborative efforts to develop an integrated social science.

Strangely enough, however, this new spirit has not yet found its way into literature dealing with the history of sociology. The history of sociology in France seems to begin with Comte and to culminate in Durkheim. One has the impression that Max Weber wrote only on the Protestant ethic and ideal types. It reminds one of the facetious remark that Beethoven wrote three symphonies – the 1st, the 5th and the 9th.

All European countries have conducted empirical social research for nearly 200 years. As a matter of fact, many of the techniques which are now considered American in origin were developed in Europe 50 or 100 years ago and then were exported from the United States after they had been refined and made manageable for use on a mass scale.

In order to place the history of sociology in its correct perspective it is necessary to recapture the history of empirical research and to add it to the existing histories of social concepts and theories. A group of young scholars in the Department of Sociology of Columbia University is now working on this rediscovery; the present volume is part of this effort. It points out with considerable insight what empirical work in the modern sense the Germans did between the creation of the German Empire and the beginning of the first World War. The reader will find surprising facts as well as topics to puzzle over. Thus, for instance, it turns out that Max Weber, the patron saint of large-scale theory builders, was closely connected with quantitative investigations of contemporary social problems six times in his life. He and the scholars who worked under his direction reported at least 1000 pages of research findings which, in style and format, would not be easily distinguished from the pages of our contemporary sociological journals. But, while much of Weber's general writings have been translated into many other languages, his empirical work is virtually unknown outside Germany and probably little known even there. Tönnies, whose distinction of Gemeinschaft and Gesellschaft has remained a corner-stone of much sociological thinking, spent a good part of his life trying to promote the notion of 'sociography' and the creation of what he called 'sociological observatories.'

The question is why these efforts were not accepted as a legitimate part of sociology by the German universities. Mr. Oberschall gives us the facts and tries to explain them in terms of institutional and cultural resistances. His interpretations permit us to recast our picture of the history of German sociology; in addition he makes a fine contribution to the sociology of knowledge itself. Thus, he raises a number of interesting methodological questions. There were German professors trained to make the most subtle conceptual distinctions; but when it came to writing questionnaires or presenting statistical findings they used crude and sloppy procedures. For a long time it was taken for granted that one could not interview low-income people directly – it was thought necessary to use informants who were assumed to know something about their conditions. Occasionally a man like Schapper-Armedt wrote critical comments; but he had little influence because he did not belong to the academic establishment. Scholars concerned with the sociology of knowledge usually concen-trate on the history of the natural sciences. The present volume provides material which permits us to turn to our own past for socio-logical analysis.

Mr. Oberschall exercised great skill in selecting from a vast amount of unknown or forgotten publications those pieces which highlight specific methodological problems or crucial historical episodes, or ambivalence to be found among historical figures themselves. At the same time he has indicated the direction which further investigations on German material might take. Similar studies are now under way on the history of empirical social research in other countries. A volume on France is nearing completion, and comparable work in England, the United States, and to a limited extent, Italy is now under scrutiny.

The program as it is now conceived proceeds on three levels. First, what is the intrinsic development of research ideas and techniques from one period to the next? Second, what are the social networks – institutions, personal contacts, controversies – within which progress was promoted or hindered? Finally, what are the broad cultural and historical factors that shaped the birth and growth of empirical social research as we know it today?

It is legitimate to ask what utility such historical work might have. In one respect this is a question which can only be answered by the truism that knowledge of the past helps in understanding the present. But the several approaches adopted by Mr. Oberschall permits one to be somewhat more specific. The most obvious applications are connected with the second approach – the institutional aspect. We have not yet found the appropriate place for empirical social research on the contemporary scene. In the universities we have makeshift arrangements like bureaus and institutes; but these are not really integrated with the teaching tradition of the social sciences. Outside the universities there are commercial agencies which have undefined relations to academic work and there are government agencies which cannot obtain adequate personnel because the universities do not yet provide the kind of training which, say, students of medicine or law get through their professional schools. There can be no doubt that institutional experiences provide guidance for more recent efforts toward innovation.

The third approach – interpretation of research traditions in terms of the broad social context – is, of course, the most difficult one. It will require collaboration between historians and social scientists to explain the conditions under which empirical social research is accepted and why such strong discontinuities occurred in the past 200 years. But once more light is shed on these factors, it will be seen that they have implications for the transfer of experience from one place to another, including now the underdeveloped countries; more accurate predictions will result.

For the first approach – the intrinsic history of ideas – it is most difficult to make a claim for direct utility; but, hopefully, here it is perhaps least necessary. I am confident that the general reader will be quite fascinated by finding in the following pages examples of the way in which modern techniques grew, how at first they were only dimly perceived and how long it took before a clear methodological

selfawareness developed. The professional social scientist will undoubtedly find himself stimulated by Dr. Oberschall's examples to find
in his own work similar trends which he otherwise would have over-
looked, and his selfconfidence will increase when he becomes aware
that his techniques have a distinguished past. It is therefore appropriate to close this introduction with an expression of thanks to the
present author and of hope that other colleagues will want to analyze
further the rich material available on the history of empirical social
research.

PAUL F. LAZARSFELD

Acknowledgements

This book was written while I was at the Bureau of Applied Social Research at Columbia University, and was circulated in limited form as a mimeographed report from the Bureau. I have made some changes and additions to the text of that report.

I want to thank professors Juan Linz, Fritz Stern, Hans Zetterberg, and Rudolf Heberle for their helpful criticism. I owe a debt of gratitude to Professor Paul F. Lazarsfeld who first called the topic to my attention, and who subsequently as principal advisor guided me through the difficulties I encountered.

I wish to thank the International Social Science Council and the École Pratique des Hautes Études (Sorbonne) for making this publication possible.

ANTHONY OBERSCHALL

Table of contents

I. *Introduction*

In a recent paper on the history of quantification in sociology, Paul F. Lazarsfeld [82] discussed some trends and problems in the works of the English political arithmeticians, the descriptive statisticians in the German universities, the Belgian astronomer Quetelet who was the first to apply mathematical models to social data, and of Le Play and his school. The present work is intended to trace the origin and development of social research in Germany along the broad lines set down by Lazarsfeld. The approach will be both descriptive and critical. A faithful picture of the kinds of research undertaken will be presented, but the emphasis will be on the methodology of the studies and on problems of quantification. A great part of the discussion will be therefore devoted to the manner of conceptualizing a certain problem and how that was subsequently incorporated into a research design, questionnaire or other procedures. Actual findings will be reported only if, as in the case of Levenstein's survey of working class attitudes, they are valuable historical documents. The emphasis is thus on constructive criticism, an attempt to show how certain problems were approached and successfully solved, or on the contrary what errors were made and how since that time similar difficulties have been met by other research procedures.

An interesting aspect of this history is the near-institutionalization of social research at several points between 1848 and 1914. Yet a case study such as this can only attempt to yield a provisional and tentative answer to this puzzling question. Only when similar studies of the history of social research in Britain, France, Italy, the Low Countries and Scandinavia have prepared the groundwork, will the historian of empirical social science be able to draw up that combination of factors which was necessary and or sufficient to bring about the institutionalization of social research and the directions it took. Generalizations based on a single case are always hazardous and often misleading. In the conclusion, an attempt will nonetheless be made to bring together a number of facts made at scattered places all bearing on this question and to present a tentative explanation of why empirical social research did not become established in Germany as an ongoing and continuous enterprise.

The set of activities included under the notion of empirical social research will be somewhat narrower than many social scientists normally include in that term. Purely historical research on social and economic matters, which represents the greater part of the total amount of research carried out by the German social scientists in the period 1848-1914, will not be included in the discussion. The activities of the psychological laboratories and physical anthropological measurements and its problematics will not be considered either. Lastly, and perhaps more difficult to justify, the activities which went under the name of ethnography, ethnology, and *Völkerpsychologie*, and which were loosely based on material from the study of languages, myths, the history of religions and primitive cultures will also be excluded. The main reason is that in Germany this line of investigation did not join forces with the emerging discipline of sociology as it was slowly breaking away from the historical school of economics and from philosophy, unlike France where in the work of Durkheim and his school, the anthropological, social psychological and sociological lines of thought met and remained bound up with each other. As the social psychologist Willy Hellpach has observed [59, p. 53]: 'From Herder and Wilhelm von Humboldt through Lazarus and Steinthal to Wilhelm Wundt, Volk-psychology has remained essentially linguistics if we note that the examination of myths, fairy tales, songs, poetry and the drama also had at their foundation a common concern for language. Wundt's classical lectures on 'Völkerpsychologie' at the University of Leipzig, which have exerted such an extraordinary influence upon the study of the collective mentality of peoples and nations all over the world, devoted as a rule over half of the semester to language, barely one third to myth, and everything else (custom, law, work, technology, economy, the state) was compressed into two or three hours.'[1] Even with these exclusions, the volume and scope of empirical

---

[1] Lazarus, a linguist, and Steinthal, a philosopher, edited from 1860 to 1890 the *Zeitschrift für Völkerpsychologie und Sprachwissenschaften*, which in its early years included many articles by the editors still written in Hegelian terminology, as well as contributions by the jurist Paul Laband, the philosopher and educator Friedrich Paulsen, and the moral statistician Etienne Laspeyres. Later the journal became

social research, which was carried out in the period 1848-1914 mainly by professional political economists at the universities and by an assortment of innovators without an academic background, will surprise many who have been accustomed to take the notion of the predominantly historical orientation of 19th century German social science for granted. The terminal date of 1914 which sets an artificial boundary to the period under discussion will be disregarded in many instances where a continuity in social research into the post-war years is evident, although as a rule only an outline and references will be indicated in footnotes.

Large scale social surveys by means of questionnaires were a commonplace means of social factfinding in Germany before the first World War. All the leading historical economists, Schmoller, Bücher, Brentano, Adolph Wagner, as well as those of the next generation who are known to us as the founders of sociology, Tönnies and Max Weber, became involved in planning and directing surveys, writing out questionnaires and analyzing the returns. The origin of the social survey in Germany can be traced back to the material and social upheaval brought about by the industrial revolution. The purpose of most surveys was to find out what the material and moral condition of the working classes was. The motivation behind them was unmistakably the desire for reform and legislation. In broad outline these developments followed with a 40-year lag the events in France, with one important difference. In France it was reform minded physicians, philanthropists, and even socialist newspapers that first conducted working class surveys in the years preceding the revolution of 1848. The French government had conducted before that time only investigations in specific industries. Then only under the pressure of the mob during the confusing revolutionary days of

_____

concerned exclusively with language and myth. In 1925 the journal *Zeitschrift für Völkerpsychologie und Soziologie* appeared under the direction of Richard Thurnwald. In the first article of the new journal Thurnwald called attention to the important differences with the earlier *Zeitschrift*. *Völkerpsychologie* as it was developed by Lazarus and Steinthal had been still closely allied with the philosophy of history. They had used such concepts as *Volksgeist* and collective soul not merely as convenient constructs, but as objective entities divorced from social influences. Thurnwald's own notion of the discipline was on the other hand close to present day cultural anthropology and social psychology. A history of social research in the post-war period would not be able to exclude the activities carried out under the banner of ethnography and *Völkerpsychologie* as we have done for the 1848-1914 period.

1848 in Paris, did it set out to organize its first *enquête ouvrière* [114]. In England too the pioneers of social surveys were physicians, clergymen, and other well-to-do reformers who carried out their work outside the universities and the government. In Germany the idea of conducting social surveys originated directly from the bureaucracy and the university professors who were mockingly known as the 'socialists of the chair.' Some leading men from both groups belonged to the same organization, the *Verein für Sozialpolitik*, that unique association of reform minded men, part professional association, part pressure group. On the occasion of the first great German survey of factory workers and apprentices conducted in 1875 by the bureaucracy on behalf of the Reichstag, they had the examples of English, French and Belgian surveys to draw from, and all three models were widely discussed. Despite this auspicious start of the survey in the hands of professionals and their subsequent use of it, it did not become perfected as an instrument of social research. The reasons for this are many and will receive detailed attention.

Whereas the social survey was a consciously borrowed import from France, there existed in Germany a much older academic tradition of 'statistics'. It was a curious mixture of geography, administrative law and political theory. It consisted of descriptive accounts of states, their people and government, their customs and industry, presented in the form of complex classificatory systems. Its origins have been traced back to Conring in the 17th century [82]. Subsequently men like Achenwall in Göttingen and Schlözer were its foremost exponents. This tradition recognized the usefulness of 'statistical' voyages in the manner of Arthur Young and the Marquis de Custine 'that allow one to observe first hand the people, the constitution and the government and their influence on life, customs and behavior' [72, p. 122]. One of the last men to carry out such trips in Germany was W. H. Riehl in the 1850s and 1860s. He strongly advocated the field trip and direct observation as the foundation of an empirical science of the state. Despite his great popular success Riehl never succeeded in this endeavor. After him this long tradition became fragmented into areas such as geography and physical anthropology.

By the 1850s the numerical statisticians had succeeded in displacing the descriptive statisticians. The new science of political economy was introduced into the universities and its right hand was the demographic and economic data which was by this time regularly collected and turned out by the government statistical agencies. Adolphe Quetelet's international fame had in the meanwhile conferred respectability upon those who wished to work analytically with numerical data. For two decades in the 1860s and 1870s moral statistics became an exciting field of new ideas and controversy in Germany. Wilhelm Lexis all but introduced the idea of a mathematical model of mass behavior. Yet this tradition eventually fizzled out. At the end of the century moral statistics had become but another form of social bookkeeping in the hands of Georg von Mayr. In dozens of articles over much of his academic life, Tönnies tried to revive interest in an analytic treatment of social statistical data.[2] He investigated the association between ecological variables and between time series in order to arrive inductively at quantitative laws on suicide, criminal behavior, even electoral behavior. His ambition was to achieve a synthesis between the older, qualitatively rich, descriptive statistics and the exact analysis of numerical data. He conceived of this synthesis as a broad empirical foundation for sociology and called it 'sociography.' Tönnies did not succeed in getting his colleagues interested. His own achievements in this area were not commensurate with his efforts. Tönnies did not succeed in bringing his theoretical concepts to bear on his numerical computations. He almost relapsed into a form of radical empiricism in his work with social statistics.

In the eighties and nineties when moral statistics had faded as a novelty, it was the political economists in the Verein für Sozialpolitik who became the center for social research with their social surveys of peasants and land-laborers. The early surveys were not at all what is today meant by that term. The respondents to whom the circulars or questionnaires were sent were third parties, such as officials, teachers, ministers, landowners, members of local government or local associations, or other men who were thought to be well-informed on the conditions of the peasantry in their area. These informants would send back their answers usually in the form of an essay. The fundamental problem of how to analyze and present these returns in summary form was never satisfactorily solved during this period. Often the essays were merely reproduced *in extenso*. In the end the initiators of the survey would summarize the findings in dramatic

---

[2] Much of Tönnies' social statistical work was published after the War, but since it was a continuation of the type of analysis he had started around the turn of the century, it will receive detailed treatment.

speeches at the Verein meetings at which the policy implications were stressed and alternative solutions to social problems discussed and debated. It was hardly an appropriate setting for raising matter-of-fact methodological issues. The general lack of interest in improvement of the instruments used was especially evident in questionnaire construction. Sometimes the very questions that were declared unusable, vague, biased or awkward by investigators who had used them first were repeated word for word in a later survey. The leading Verein members did not engage in methodological criticism of surveys and no one made it his business to publish a manual or compilation of principles and examples useful in questionnaire and survey design. The Verein surveys did not result in the improvement of social research methods.

Whereas the historical economists of the Verein für Sozialpolitik were concerned primarily with economic conditions, once the fever of empirical research spread among religious organizations, the topic of investigation shifted to the moral condition and psychology of the working class. This shift corresponded to some extent to a change in the problems of the working class. It was no longer the question of pauperism and gradual impoverishment which was foremost, but that of social and moral disruption from factory and city life, even while lower class political consciousness and strength were on the rise. The pioneer of these research developments was the young theology student Paul Göhre, who in 1890 spent three months working incognito in a machine tool factory in Chemnitz and during the remaining hours fully shared the life of his fellow workers. The book in which he described his experiences made a great impression and might still today be cited as an example of an objective and perceptive field report. Two years later Göhre and Max Weber conducted a large survey of ministers on the condition of rural laborers on behalf of the Evangelical-Social Congress. Weber considered the survey complementary to a Verein survey on the same topic in 1891-92 in which he had taken an active part and distinguished himself. Other religious bodies followed the example of the Congress. One such survey on the morals and morality of the rural lower classes was an early version of a Kinsey report.

The period after 1900 was characterized by diversification in social research. The university professors working either in the Verein or through their seminars no longer dominated the scene, topics became more limited but received intensive treatment, and institutional records were being analyzed. The innovators came from many walks of life. The physicist, industrialist, and philanthropist Ernst Abbe performed a careful experiment on the effect of shortening working hours in the Zeiss optical works. The librarian Walter Hofmann attempted to find differences between middle-class and lower-class psychology from the records of books taken out from a public library. Richard Ehrenberg, an economist critical of the dominant historical school, dug into the records of the Krupp steel works to trace trends in the life-situation of three generations of workers and to compute exact social mobility rates. Numerous studies of elites and of occupational strata were undertaken, often under the influence of Social Darwinism which contributed heavily to the intellectual climate both in the universities and outside. Ecological studies of voting based on election statistics were also performed, and the entire institution of higher learning and particularly the universities became the object of social statistical investigations. The most spectacular achievement was, however, that of the self-educated worker Adolf Levenstein, who in 1907 undertook single-handedly the first great attitude survey on record and in many ways obtained the most successful results of all the German surveys before the war with over 5,000 answers by fellow workers. For several years Levenstein refused to analyze and publish the results until Max Weber, who had seen parts of the raw data, managed to persuade him to that effect. Levenstein eventually spent months of coding and tabulating and in some ways followed Weber's advice on how a socialpsychological survey ought to be analyzed. On the final page of the book in which he published the results in 1912, Levenstein drew up a balance of indictment of bourgeois society: on one side of the page he added up from all the questions he had asked to total number of answers which expressed satisfaction or acquiescence of the workers to their lot in life, on the other side of the page the total number of answers expressing dissatisfaction, apathy or despair. Unfortunately Levenstein's achievement had no impact upon the academic world, perhaps because of the novelty of attitude research, and no doubt also because the war followed too closely upon it.

In the years following his famous study of the Protestant Ethic, Max Weber became immersed body and soul in problems of social research. He was the main designer of the Verein für Sozialpolitik survey of industrial workers in 1909-1911. In many ways this survey was the most carefully thought through piece of empirical research of the pre-war period. Weber spent an entire summer of observation and computation at the textile mill of a relative in preparation for it. His intention was to explore how far the conceptual apparatus and exact measurement techniques developed in the psychological sciences could be fruitfully applied to a study of industrial work on a mass scale and in a natural factory setting. It was the first explanatory survey (as opposed to the previous descriptive and fact-finding use of surveys on the material and moral condition of the working class) since it was meant to test concrete hypotheses by means of multivariate analysis. For the first time in Verein history the workers were asked in person to provide the basic data. The intent was to combine such questionnaire data with a systematic exploitation of factory records and direct observation of the workers on the factory floor. It proved far too ambitious an undertaking for the techniques and resources at hand. Despite many refinements Weber adopted the predominantly psychophysical approach of his contemporaries to problems of industrial work. The study was unfortunately doomed to failure right at its start when most of the workers refused to fill out the Verein questionnaires.

It cannot be denied, however, that despite the diversity of empirical work that was carried out in the period 1848-1914, a tradition of social research never became firmly established. Max Weber had tried to do so more than anyone else. During his life he was directly involved in three surveys and planned two additional ones in 1910 upon the foundation of the German Sociological Society. He had helped to create the Society with the hope of making available an association of professionals who would be interested in performing empirical research on a large scale. At that time he also toyed with the idea of establishing a permanent social research institute. Perhaps because his efforts in this direction remained unsuccessful, most commentators have chosen to ignore this aspect of Weber's life. Today in Germany many people are not aware of the studies that will be discussed at length below. The first world war, the premature death of Weber, the fragile empirical tradition of the twenties and finally the Nazi era have all contributed to creating a break with this aspect of the past. In the concluding chapter a systematic attempt will be made to explain why social research did not become institutionalized. In particular Max Weber's frustrations in trying to bring an enduring social research organization into being will be described in detail.

A brief look at German society is necessary at this point, for without it the surveys and studies to be described will not appear in their proper context. It is no coincidence that most of them deal substantively with working class problems and that they were primarily motivated by reform rather than scientific knowledge for its own sake. It is not suggested that social research as an intellectual product can be fully understood by merely looking at the political, social and economic transformation which was taking place. The structure of higher education, the cultural tradition in the universities and the factors usually subsumed in the elusive notion of an 'intellectual climate' are even more relevant for understanding the history of social research in Germany, and in the absence of an institutionalized tradition the part played by single individuals and their peculiarities should not be underestimated either.

In terms of political and economic change, the period 1848-1914 saw the unification of the German states into an empire under the hegemony of Prussia, and the emergence of Germany as the major military and economic power on the continent. These were years of rapid population growth and industrialization that created a tremendous growth of the cities. Germany had the largest socialist party in Europe after 1890, the Social Democratic party. The cleavage between the working class and the rest of society was quite pronounced and referred to as the 'social question', and later as the 'working class question'. Bismarck's social policy and his social insurance legislation, which were based on the idea of paternalistic responsibility, did not succeed in the end in creating a genuine national community which included the industrial workers, but it was probably responsible for the less radical direction which the socialist movement took. In addition to the rift between the cultivated and the uncultivated, the class structure of Germany was marked by the lack of a ruling class of gentlemen uniting the aristocracy, the professions, the higher civil service, and the leaders of finance and industry. Robert Lowie aptly observed that [92, p. 56] 'one modern educated German did not recognize his peer in another, but saw in him the member of a specific rank and status group, and he appraised him accordingly.' The Germans were especially fond of accentuating differences in status by means of honorary titles. University degrees and diplomas were valuable possessions for a successful career in business and government.

The intellectual scene was dominated by rapid advances in the natural, biological and historical sciences, whereas in the broader cultural context there was a decline of German arts and letters that was noted by such varied critics as Jacob Burckhardt, Friedrich Nietzsche, and Paul de Lagarde. Yet in the years after 1890 a complex intellectual period was taking shape which the American historian H. Stuart Hughes has characterized as [69, p. 51] a 'cultural revival' and the beginning of a 'secession of the intellectuals,' and the German historian Georg Steinhausen has described as [132, Chap. I] a widespread feeling of 'cultural superiority' together with a 'mood of decline.' Because the universities played such a dominant role in the intellectual and scientific life of the country, it is necessary to examine the social structure of higher education somewhat in greater detail, for its operation goes a long way in explaining the stimuli and barriers to the development of social research and the ways in which it was organized.

The intellectual and scientific life of Germany was not shaped by a scientific and literary elite unaffiliated with institutions of higher learning as was the case in some other countries. There was no parallel in Germany to a Darwin or a Galton. The university professor in Germany on the other hand enjoyed the highest prestige, because of the high value placed on education in German culture and because the universities were located mainly in small towns whose entire life and economic sustenance depended upon them. There was considerable rivalry among the university towns and the states in which they were located to acquire the top professors and to outshine each other. In the 19th century the higher educational system of Germany was considered the finest in the world. Many foreign students came there to complete their studies. The university professors were an extremely hard working and productive group, whose highest duty was the advancement of science in a tradition of careful scholarship. There were, however, a number of important problems that were already noted by contemporaries. First, the tradition of scholarship centering on library research, archives, and the seminars were tending towards overspecialization to the detriment of broad learning. Second, the mechanism of appointments and promotions, with the faculties recommending and the ministries of education approving the candidates, led such men as Max Weber to state that [169, p. 132] 'chance rather than ability ruled' in the choices, and that he was surprised at the number of correct appointments that were in the end made in spite of the system. Third, most of the professors came from a patrician and middle class background. By their own inclination and awareness of the social transformation taking place around them, their sympathies were for social reform and legislation to improve the lot of the workers and peasants, yet as employees of the state and members of the upper middle class they had loyalties and obligations which were at times pulling in a different direction. As H. Stuart Hughes has written [69, pp. 49-50]: 'The German intellectual of the Wilhelmian era was in a peculiar ambiguous relationship to his own political and social milieu... a tension between political acceptance and opposition.' Lastly, the style of academic pursuit had a strong critical and even negative element in it. The personal polemics and rivalries between the various schools often prevented scientific controversies from being settled according to objective criteria and from being restricted to the specific issues at hand. According to the historian Franz Schnabel [121, III, p. 138], 'The polemics in the universities often exceeded to the joy of the students the imaginable limits of personal insults; the heads of schools and their followers always faced each other fully armed for battle.'

The German historical school of economics, which in the period 1848-1914 carried out much of the social research that will be discussed below and which became the most important contributor to the emerging discipline of sociology, was characterized by a high rate of productivity as well as its share of numerous disputes and controversies, or 'Streiten' as they were called.[3] It is convenient to make the distinction between four 'generations' of economists and social scientists, for they often tended to take up opposing positions. The oldest generation was made up of the founders of the historical school, Roscher, Knies, Hildebrand and the statistician Engel. The second generation and one which was to play an important role in the development of social research was made up of Schmoller, Brentano,

---

[3] Around the turn of the century, there were about a dozen social science journals and periodical series (excluding purely historical journals) which were filled by the contributions of no more than about eitghty professional economists and social scientitsts. These journals, incidentally, also served the function of providing each rival faction with a ready organ to state its point of view and carry on polemics.

Knapp, Bücher, Wagner, Conrad and Lexis. The third generation contained the founding fathers of German sociology, Weber, Tönnies, Simmel, Sombart, and Troeltsch, and finally the fourth generation, which is mentioned only in a marginal way because its period of activity unfolded mainly in the post-war years, was made up of such diverse men as Michels and Lukács.

There were at least seven major issues that were the center of a great deal of controversy, although it is artificial to treat them independently of each other since one of the distinguishing marks of the period was precisely the way in which conflicting issues spilled over into neighboring side-issues and expanded into personal polemics and rivalries. First, there was the historical orientation of economics in Germany which was due to the rejection by the oldest generation of the British school of classical economics, and which the second generation accentuated to the point of international isolation from the mainstream of developing economic theory [128, p. 142]. The main controversy here was between Gustav Schmoller and the head of the Austrian school, Carl Menger, the one emphasizing the historical case study approach because of the uniqueness of real economic systems, the other stressing an analytic approach using abstract models indispensable for an exact science. This was to some extent related to the second and more famous controversy that dealt with the difference between the natural and the cultural-historical sciences, and which was basically a philosophical issue. The second generation was less concerned with it, but the third generation, especially Max Weber, played a decisive role in this controversy which was often referred to simply as the *Methodenstreit*. This issue was also associated with a division along geographical lines separating the Southwest school from Northern Germany. Others in the third generation like Sombart turned to Marx for their inspiration for a basic methodological position. The third controversy was that between economic liberalism and state intervention and tariff protectionism, which in 1872 led directly to the creation of the Verein für Sozialpolitik, but which soon died down except for occasional flare-ups because free competition was sacrificed everywhere in Europe with the spread of trusts, monopolies and the economic competition between the major powers. More important was the fourth controversy about one's position on the social, or working class, question. It involved support of various political parties, attitudes towards the socialists, the trade unions, the government bureaucracy, as well as one's disposition towards Prussian dominance in Germany. Schmoller and Brentano for years were not on speaking terms with each other because they disagreed precisely on the social question, and this was also true of the hostile attitude of Wagner and Brentano to each other. All of them in turn differed from the third generation, especially Weber, who took a sharper and much more positive stand on the primacy of national power over the working class question. The fifth major controversy on a value-free social science, the *Wertfreiheitstreit*, was not unrelated to the preceding issue. In general most professors were agreed that science ought to be non-partisan and that it could not settle questions about what ought to be, but in practice the second generation was especially fond of preaching and propagandizing from the university classroom, which earned them the mocking designation of 'socialists of the chair.' The third generation reacted strongly against these practices, again the reaction was strongest in Weber, and they were led to create the German Sociological Society as a strictly professional association as one way in which to circumvent their elders' ethical and political commitments. The fourth generation of Michels and Lukács tended to revert again to a union of scientific pursuit and political commitment. The sixth controversy was of an academic nature and was a consequence of the intellectual division of labor, the scarcity of university positions and the prestige accorded to the various disciplines. It was the conflict of the emergence and breaking away of new fields of inquiry from their mother disciplines. Sociology did not get officially recognized as an independent field until after the war when the first professorships of sociology were established. It is important to remember that it was not alone in trying to secure recognition in the faculties. There were ethnography, anthropology, *Völkerkunde*, social psychology, social biology, demography, social geography, the science of social masses and several other overlapping fields of inquiry, being pushed by this or that man and his students, competing against each other and fighting the established disciplines of philosophy, economics, and history. Finally there was a purely generational conflict about access to the limited number of professorial positions and the low level of remuneration for the lowest level of university teachers, the *Privatdozenten*, and which involved such specific issues as the establishment of a mandatory age of retirement for the full professors who tended to be an extremely longlived group.

While these controversies of the two decades preceding the outbreak of the First World War were decisive in shaping an intellectual and cultural climate in which sociology as a discipline distinct from philosophy, history, and economics had considerable difficulty emerging, their impact upon the development of empirical research was not of the same order of importance.[4] This was so because controversies such as the *Methodenstreit* were carried out on a philosophical plane completely removed and without reference to the more simple, basically fact-finding, social research activities that some of the protagonists in the debates were concurrently engaged in. Weber's solution to the problem of generalization from unique historical data by means of ideal types, which he conceived of as abstract limiting concepts not necessarily found in their total purity, but containing the essential features of real social phenomena (as was for example his notion of 'rational action') did not prevent him from suggesting to Levenstein an inductive typological procedure for quantitative empirical data which had no relation to the notion of ideal types, and which was in fact quite similar to current procedures (see Chap. V, sec. 8, below). When Weber in a polemical speech at the 1909 Verein für Sozialpolitik convention and on other occasions described the actual operation of bureaucracies, he certainly discussed it in terms which went beyond and even contradicted his ideal type formulation (see Chap. VI, sec. 6. below). On the other hand it might be argued that Weber's notion of historical explanation, of *verstehen*, which involved an intuitive understanding for human motivation and attitudes, did influence his approach to the question of how the attitudes and motivations of industrial workers ought to be ascertained and combined with other variables bearing on their productivity such as the level of wages, the length of the working day and the temperature and humidity on the factory floor (see Chap. VI, sec. 3 below). Perhaps the most decisive consequence of the *Methodenstreit* for social research was that the concrete methodology and technology of social research was left neglected in favor of abstract and philosophical arguments. Finally it should be mentioned, and it will be pointed out in the appropriate places, that a man like Weber did not segregate his historical and cultural studies

---

[4] For an excellent account of this period from the point of view of intellectual history, see H. Stuart Hughes [69]. For a complete and technical exposition of the major *Methodenstreit* and its numerous ramifications, that on the natural and cultural sciences, see Felix Kaufmann [73].

from the empirical social research activities he was also engaged in, but that on the contrary there exist cross-references between these two lines of scientific pursuit and instances where Weber applied some contemporary findings as evidence in the explanation of historically remote events.

II. *Social surveys up to 1895*

1. *The early surveys*

The basic questions which need clarification in order to understand the beginnings of German social survey work and the direction it took are first, why the Germans adopted the French and Belgian form of social surveys, the *enquête*, even though praising the superiority of the British Royal Commission as a means of social investigation; second, why the relevant information was invariably extracted through the agency of three parties[1]; and finally, why the surveys were organized geographically so as to embrace at least a report from every region or county of Germany. Surveys limited in topic as well as in geographical extension are not characteristic of the period before 1900.

These questions can be answered satisfactorily by examining the discussions centering on the methods of organizing social surveys which took place in the Verein für Sozialpolitik in 1877 as a prelude to the first Verein survey. One discussant, Embden, defines 'survey' as [39, p. 3] '...an undertaking, authorized by law, to ascertain economic and social facts and their causal relationships, the ultimate purpose of which is *the preparation of legislative or administrative acts*, and which is accomplished primarily by interrogation of witnesses and knowledgeable men.' Embden recognizes that there are private surveys, surveys by organizations other than the government, carried out for primarily scientific reasons by means of questionnaires, but he assigns them a very secondary significance.[2] The purpose of surveys is then eminently practical. It is supposed to help the legislator and the administrator in their task of good government. This basic purpose meant necessarily that the surveys had to cover all the territory of Germany, for laws such as the factory-inspection law also applied to all of it, and indeed defined the character of these early surveys as

---

[1] Variously called 'Vertrauensmänner' or 'Sachverständigen.'
[2] Similarly 20 years later in 1895, Georg von Mayr [98, I, p. 8] played down the role of privately organized surveys. For him 'statistics' was still synonymous with census-type, exhaustive fact-gathering carried out by and for the government.

geographically organized and analyzed, descriptive and fact-finding.

These considerations bring us close to answering also the first question, why the questionnaire survey typical of France and Belgium was adopted, rather than the small fact-finding body which held hearings, cross-examined witnesses, and made on-the-spot inspection trips that was so characteristic of England and which fulfilled the same functions of fact-finding and opinion sounding before new legislation was introduced. Germany had a well functioning, geographically decentralized bureaucracy. It had capable men in local offices accustomed to help the census in the manner of the *intendants* in France. On the other hand, the people at large had not the tradition of taking part in the affairs of government that England had established at an early date. Embden [39, p. 8] drew a parallel between the form of government and the form of the fact-finding bodies in the two countries. In a bureaucratic state 'it is good for the well being of the state if, from time to time, it finds out where the loyal citizen's shoes are pinching,' whereas in a parliamentary form of government 'the citizen stands watch to find out whether laws, administrative measures and public servants need rectification and regulation.' Hence in Germany the questionnaires sent to officials and local dignitaries who reported conscientiously on local conditions, but with no checks from the side of the objects of the investigation, and in England the Royal Commission with its active participation of citizens in many walks of life, where the oral testimony of one could be checked against the statements of some other witness on the spot.

The discussions about the relative advantages of the French and the English type survey unfortunately centered on legal and organizational matters rather than on the scientific design of surveys. The social scientists' energies were engaged in thinking through the best way to organize a survey – should there be extensive stenographic reports or condensed essays based on them, should there be one man or a team investigating in a locality and what should his training be, should the material be analyzed centrally or already partly locally – whereas hardly anyone paid attention to how a questionnaire should be constructed, which questions could be expected to be answered on basis of fact and not mere guesswork, what was to be done with the raw data once it had been obtained, in short, all the questions which today are grouped under the heading of 'design' and 'analysis' of surveys.

There had been administrative surveys in Germany before the 1870s, but these were conducted on a small, regional scale as a response to conditions resulting from natural calamities. The year preceding the 1848 revolutions in Germany was marked by crop failures throughout the country. In Prussia, the Royal Commission for Agriculture, under the direction of Alexander von Lengerke [85] undertook a survey of the condition of the rural laboring classes by sending questionnaires to agricultural associations. Questions included such items as budget breakdown for a typical family, the level of wages, and the ability of the peasants to provide adequately for their family needs. No attempt was made to analyze the returns in a quantitative manner [41, p. 18]. In the same year in Saxony, a commission appointed by the minister of the interior sent out a circular containing over 300 questions. To illustrate the nature of these administrative surveys, questions 70-74 of the Saxony commission are reproduced in full. 'Is the condition of the workers susceptible to improvement? Which classes are the most favored by fate, which the most oppressed? What is the relationship of income to life needs? What are the higher and lower pleasures of life? What is the state of family life? Of education and child rearing? Of morals? What are the chances for a worker of becoming independent (self-employed)?' [41, pp. 20-21]. These questions were impossible to answer precisely nor was this probably their primary aim. The minister of the interior meant to be kept up to date on important local developments such as economic hardship and signs of popular discontent. Questions such as these served in fact as an outline by means of which the local informant was reminded of the points upon which to base his evaluation of local social and economics conditions. The fate of the Saxony survey is not entirely clear. Because of the political reaction following the revolution and the good crop of 1849, the returned questionnaires were probably filed away and forgotten.[3]

---

[3]   The author is acquainted with both of these studies only from the secondary source [41]. The administrative surveys, hearings and investigations which were carried out by various ministries for their own information before the drafting of legislation and which as a rule were not published, are not included in this history of social research. Such collecting of information is, of course, characteristic of any bureaucracy, public or private, and there is a thin line indeed between what one might include under social research and what not. Especially in the period 1873-1880 when Bismarck's social insurance legislation was being drafted and perfected in various government agencies and ministries, many fact-finding and opinion

The first national survey in Germany was actually a mixture of the French and English type. It was conducted by the bureaucracy in 1875 on behalf of the Reichstag in order to find out what the conditions were like in the factories, especially for apprentices. Although the report [111] is rather sketchy on precisely what procedures were used, apparently civil servants held hearings in more than 500 localities where they orally questioned close to 7,000 informants, 2/3 of them factory owners and managers, the remaining 1/3 workers, by asking them some two dozen questions reproduced on pages 10-14 of the report. The intent of the survey was to find out how far the factory legislation passed in 1872-1873 was being observed or evaded. Typical questions asked were whether or not the factory was closed on Sundays and holidays. Compared to government surveys in Europe at that time, this one was not an ambitious undertaking. Both the 1868-1869 Belgian survey on conditions in the mines and the 1872 French survey of factory workers were more elaborate and better designed. Such surveys had by the 1870s acquired an almost standard form. There were the inevitable questions on child and woman labor, on hygienic conditions, on wages, on the nature of the labor contract, on the length of the working day, on seasonal unemployment, on accidents and accident prevention. Often an additional section was included on a typical worker's family budget, on mutual aid societies, on literacy, education, and the inevitable final question on the moral, intellectual, and physical condition of the workers and how it compared with conditions twenty years earlier.[4] The German survey of 1875 did not aim as high as this, and no attempt was made to analyze the results quantitatively.

A more ambitious and successful undertaking was the 1874-75 survey of agricultural laborers conducted by Theodor von der Goltz on behalf of the Congress of German Landowners [54]. The Congress

---

sounding activities were performed among workers, tradesmen, factory managers, landowners, merchants and local administrations [154, pp. 29, 56]. Most of these are available only in the Archives of the respective ministries. It would be interesting to find out in what manner and by whom the data were analyzed, and whether these activities had any influence upon the surveys carried out by academic economists.

[4] The questionnaire which Marx drew up in 1880 for the periodical *Revue Socialiste* was also of this basic form. Marx's last question, #100, read: 'What is the general physical, intellectual and moral condition of the men and women workers employed in your trade?' For a convenient reprint of the questionnaire, see Bottomore [20, pp. 204-212].

sent out 15,000 questionnaires to landowners all over Germany, and a roughly 20% return was obtained. The questionnaires (pp. viii-xi) were of two basic types: (A) on income primarily, with 24 questions, and (B) on 'other conditions,' with 12 questions numbered 25 through 36. (B) represented an interesting innovation with respect to the standard type of agricultural survey since an attempt was made to cover an area other than the strictly material condition of the peasants and laborers. Question #25 read: 'Is there a tendency among laborers to save money in order to be able to buy their own plot of land later on? Does this tendency appear already among the unmarried workers or only after marriage?' Question #29 was the inevitable one on the 'material, intellectual, and moral' condition of the laborers, but in #31 an attempt was made to respecify it by seeking information on the increase of theft, drunkenness, illegitimacy rate, and standard of living as compared to 10 or 20 years earlier. Other questions included items on the spread of socialist propaganda and agitation, the use of public libraries if they were available, and emigration.[5]

The great weakness of these questions was that they assumed a thorough knowledge of the laborers' daily lives on the part of the landlords and a scientifically detached attitude in the case of those who somehow did have access to such information. Goltz naturally was aware of this when he wrote, in the introduction, that the results were satisfactory with respect to the questions on the material conditions of the laborers, but 'where, for the information sought in a question, a subjective evaluation or judgment was called for, as in the question on the material, intellectual and moral development of the workers, reports, even within relatively small counties are often contradictory.' Furthermore all the questions were open-ended, even those that were eminently quantifiable, such as #31 on the changes in the frequency of theft, etc. As it turned out, the answers to such questions were unusable, since a simple answer of 'yes' or 'no' to #31 does not yield any absolute numerical value essential for comparisons between counties.

Goltz did not know quite what to do with the data he had obtained, and in the end merely summarized the content of all 36 questions, county by county, for 450 pages. He did not attempt to synthesize the data in tables, and the few pages at the end of the report devoted

---

[5] Many of these questions were repeated verbatim in a similar survey of agricultural workers conducted by the Verein für Sozialpolitik in 1891.

to the analysis of the findings might well have been written by someone who had not conducted a survey, but had instead travelled throughout the country, talked to the local officials, looked up already available statistics, and then written an essay on the plight of the rural working class.

2. The Verein für Sozialpolitik

In the 1880s and 1890s it was the Verein für Sozialpolitik which became the center of survey research in Germany. It was founded in 1872 by a group of reform minded professors, publishers, civil servants and even a few industrialists. Attempts to co-opt prominent trade union leaders and Social Democrats failed, and the socialist press subsequently looked upon the Verein's activities with suspicion, if not hostility, despite the Verein's active support of a better lot for the working class. In time the professorial element came to predominate in the Verein, and the nature of the organization changed from a pressure group to a professional association without ever successfully overcoming its basic ambivalence. The immediate cause which led to its foundation was a split among the German economists between the advocates of *laisser faire* and those for state intervention in matters of factory, trade union and other reform legislation [23, p. 82]. The *laisser faire* group, or those inspired by the Manchester school, were in control of the Congress of German Economists and had also easy access to the press and political parties. Their opponents, later called the 'socialists of the chair,' felt the need for a separate organization through which they too would influence public opinion and legislation. They realized that the gap between the industrial workers and the rest of society could only be mended by the intervention of the state; at the same time they rejected the Marxist solution of the German socialists [17, Chap.1].

It was almost inevitable that serious differences of opinion should develop among the leading Verein members since they covered a wide range in the political spectrum. In its first decade the Verein held yearly conventions at which important legislative questions would be thoroughly debated, and resolutions regarding them adopted by majority vote. In 1879 when Bismarck turned to a policy of protective tariffs, the internal cleavages proved too great. To save the Verein as an organization it was decided to abandon the resolutions. The main focus of Verein activity shifted to conducting investigations and surveys on contemporary problems, the results of which were discussed at the conventions now held every other year. The executive committee would decide upon the problems to be investigated, raise funds and manpower for the study and even help in designing it. In the two decades from 1881 to 1902 there were two surveys made of the condition of rural labor, one each on usury in rural areas, cottage industries, the condition of the workers engaged in trade, in peddling, in shipping, and in transport. The reason for the absence of any survey of industrial workers in these years was again due to the uneasy truce between the factions within the Verein. In the eighties while Bismarck's law against the socialists was in effect, it was less controversial to investigate rural labor instead [28, p. 122].

These surveys had more in common with the previous German surveys than with present day surveys. Usually a memorandum or circular explaining the problem at hand was drawn up by the principal investigator and reviewed by the executive committee. It would outline the points upon which information was requested from the respondents. Sometimes these points would be phrased as questions. The circular would then be sent to 'reliable' and 'knowledgeable' men spread out all over the country, and they would send back an essay on the problem as they saw it in their district, sometimes following the Verein questionnaire closely and sometimes disregarding it entirely.[6] Finally the 30 to 50 essays from all parts of Germany that were the endproduct of these surveys would be published in a series of volumes. These early efforts were rather undistinguished. The bulk of the questions referred to the material condition of the lower classes. Certainly the clumsy and vague phraseology of the questions did not help in getting exact or comparable answers.

In the 1881-83 survey of rural labor question #23 read as follows [152, XXII, p. x]: 'Is the resident population increasing? Is the number of children and child mortality a great one? Are the strength to work and bodily energy endangered by poor nourishment and overexertion? Is the age at marriage an average one or do many marriages occur at an early age?' To which the following kinds of answers were received. A minister reported that in his county[6']... the number of children is neither small nor especially great... That

___

[6] A variation used was to send the local informer several questionnaires, and he in turn would transmit them to other parties, finally base his report on their answers.

the mortality of children is especially great I have so far not noticed...'
[152, XXII, p. 185]. Another respondent who was chairman of the
local agricultural association wrote that'... even though it occurs
frequently that the laborers reach a ripe old age, many still die early
because their life has been hard and exhausting...' [152, XXIII, p.
77]. Yet another respondent observed that 'the female sex makes
every effort to get married at an early age so as to be able to work less.
In fact it is a frequently observed occurence among the Polish population here that tidy and diligent girls become sloppy, unkempt and
lazy women' [152, XXIV, p. 51]. The mixture of fact and fancy,
opinion and hearsay which makes up a good part of these answers,
even on matters upon which figures were probably available, was
typical of the early Verein für Sozialpolitik surveys.

The survey on usury in 1886-87 [152, XXXV] had a long and
confusing questionnaire as its starting point. To establish the extent
and causes of usury, as well as the processes by which some peasants
and not others became involved in it, would have taken a carefully
designed scheme including every stage of that process with specific
questions referring to each stage. The Verein questionnaire merely
suggested in question #6 a list of heterogeneous factors to be taken into
account: 'Which causes principally help in spreading all these forms of
usury? Unprofitable techniques and lack of occupational skills, economic hardship, frivolous character, bad crop, cases of accident, lack of
preparation for accidents, negligence in getting fire, hail, and life
insurance, absence of institutions extending credit, or fear of becoming
visible if one makes use of them.'

There was a lack of interest in the Verein for methodological issues.
Sweeping conclusions based on a shaky factual and methodological
foundation were often accepted quite uncritically. There existed no
book or manual at the time on how to design and carry out a survey,
and except for occasional book reviews, no methodological critiques
of surveys were undertaken.[7] The dominant note on quantification
was typically expressed by Schmoller when he wrote on the limits of
quantitative methods [120, p. 542]: 'Statistics can deal only with quantitative results; qualities, such as the most important moral and
intellectual actions, are inaccessible to it unless expressible in countable

---

[7]   In the 1909 edition of the *Handwörterbuch der Staatswissenschaften* no new reference
had been added under the entry 'Enqueten' to those already listed in the 1891
edition. In the post-war 1924 edition, the entry is omitted altogether.

events such as suicides and punished crime.'[8] Usury as a social and moral action was thought to belong to the set of qualitative phenomena inaccessible to precise calculations.

Gottlieb Schnapper-Arndt was the only Verein member who tried to overcome the general lack of concern with methodological issues. He had already been a participant in the 1881 survey of rural labor and was one of the field researchers of the usury survey. At the Verein convention at which the results of the usury survey were discussed, he was unable to persuade the discussants to look at the defects of method that in his opinion invalidated most of the reports. He thereupon published a monograph entitled *The Methodology of Social Surveys* [123], a constructive critique of the Verein survey on usury and the only document of its kind until Max Weber, much later on, became concerned with methodology in empirical research. Schnapper-Arndt thought that the participant researchers should be picked with greater care (p. 2). They usually included teachers, landowners, ministers, lawyers and members of local government, each with his own particular point of view and bias. He noted that the mere fact that the Verein conducted an investigation into usury would predispose the respondents to exaggerate the extent of the problem (p. 4). He came out strongly for neutrally worded questions and for asking only those questions which the respondents could reasonably be expected to answer on the basis of fact. He suggested that a topic not be exhausted simply by means of one long question, but that it be split into a series of interrelated questions, each with a simple 'yes' or 'no' alternative (p. 19).[9] Most of all Schnapper-Arndt deplored the lack of precision and numerical evidence in the answers. The respondents often made sweeping generalizations without citing their source, or else they would report from court records the number of complaints against usurers, omitting the percentage of court actions actually leading to convictions and the time span during which they occurred (p. 9). He noted the crude anti-semitic bias of many respondents. In answer to the question on who mainly engaged in usury,

---

[8] The juxtaposition of the words 'quantity' and 'quality,' always in opposition to each other, was probably a legacy from idealistic philosophy. Its widespread and uncritical acceptance did a great deal to keep the problem of quantification from being viewed as a question of measurement (rather than as a logical issue).
[9] This foreshadows the notion of a 'battery' of questions, a technique that has become standard practice in surveys.

he observed that (p. 40)' ... we can subdivide most of the respondents into three categories: those who make an unbiased classification; those who speak of 'also Christians'; those who report the religion only when a Jew is involved.'

Schnapper-Arndt had some interesting notions about quantification. 'In almost all branches of moral statistics, it is impossible to reach the degree of finality which one is used to in demography. For a given phenomenon whose extent one wants to capture, one must find more or less representative symptoms and delimit the area in which these symptoms are to be established statistically, although the limits might not always include the entire mass (universe).... To determine the number of unhappy marriages is impossible, but one might consider the number of divorces as a symptom of it, at any rate for purposes of comparison' [pp. 6-7]. These ideas, however loosely stated, are a precursor to the modern notion that concepts may be redefined and operationalized in terms of their indicators.[10] Schnapper-Arndt realized that court records do not yield a measure of the true extent of the practice of usury since most cases do not result in litigation, still he thought that they should be exploited systematically and numerically. Unlike Thiel, the senior investigator of the usury survey, who draws the conclusion that 'one is therefore confined to the opinion of persons who are well acquainted with the matter' [p. 10], Schnapper-Arndt suggested that in the absence of reliable institutional records the researcher should ask a number of people about their opinion, record their answers, and publish these in tabular and numerical form. He referred to this procedure as 'gathering opinion' from an 'auxiliary' group [p. 7 and p. 14].

Schnapper-Arndt's criticisms were not incorporated into the design of the subsequent Verein survey on the condition of agricultural laborers in 1891-92 [152, LIII-LV]. It was modelled after the 1874

[10] Schapper-Arndt did not consider the possibility of combining several indicators into an index. His own usage of the word 'symptom' does not differentiate between these two notions. He dimly perceived the probabilistic relationship of indicator to concept. The term 'symptom' seems to have originated in the work of the moral statisticians. Both Schnapper-Arndt and Tönnies derived it from them, yet failed to see the general applicability of indicators to social relationships and attitudes. They would have been quite surprised by the work of Burgess and Cottrel, who predicted adjustment in marriage from an index based on indicators of attitudes and social relations between the spouses. For a discussion of the issues involved, see [81, sec. I and pp. 268-276].

Goltz survey on the same topic. Many of the earlier questions were repeated *verbatim*, even those that Goltz had pointed out were poor questions. As in 1874 there were two questionnaires, one short and one long. The long questionnaire especially was a confusing document of over nine pages with no clear pattern.[11] Most of the questions dealt with the system of land tenure and the material level of living conditions, nourishment, wages, unemployment, the budget of an average family, the possibility of acquiring a plot of land. The Goltz items on socialist propaganda, public libraries, the propensity to save money and emigration were also thrown in. In short the range of subject-matter covered was roughly the same as had become customary for rural surveys since 1848. The questionnaires were again sent to proprietors and landowners all over the country. The good return which was obtained, 2,277 out of 3,180 for the long questionnaire and 291 out of 562 for the short one, indicates the prestige which the Verein by this time enjoyed. It was also the biggest survey undertaken by it up to this time.

Max Weber, who was then 27 years old and just passing his bar examinations, was called upon to analyze the reports from Eastern Germany, and from them resulted his first major work, *The Condition of the Agricultural Laborers in Germany East of the Elbe* [159]. Only he among the five Verein researchers decided to use data from the earlier 1874 and 1848 surveys, and to focus on the developmental aspect of the problem. Thirteen pages in his report (pp. 806-819) are devoted exclusively to comparative statistical tables on wages, acres owned and acres farmed, number of farm animals per family, etc., in the districts for which the information was available in the three surveys. In the main Weber followed the customary procedure of reproducing in tables only quantifiable economic items. There is no evidence to suggest that he tried to code the questions dealing with social relations and behavior. His main substantive conclusions were stated in terms of his political ideal of a powerful national state and were a clear statement of his opposition to the economic and political role of the Junkers (p. 795): 'The patriarchal giant-enterprise had been able to maintain the level of subsistence of the peasants and their military preparedness, but the capitalist type of enterprise maintains itself

---

[11]   It is no surprise that Thiel, the official head of the survey, complained that 'often the questionnaire was not understood' [152, LIII, p. xiii].

at the expense of the subsistence level, nationality and military power of the German East.'[12]

Weber's report and his dramatic presentation of the results at the Verein meetings brought him instantaneous recognition as an expert on the land question and as a sharp political mind. The survey also started Weber thinking about social research. Weber noticed that because of the lack of knowledge which the landowners had of their workers the results were uncertain at best (p. 6). He realized that the Verein, just as Goltz, had put too much emphasis on the material condition of the laborers, whereas 'the problems which the condition of the rural laborers reveal lie predominantly in the psychological area.' By that Weber meant concretely that (p. 5) 'the question is not how high the income of the workers really is, but whether as a result of (the level of wages) an orderly economy is possible for the workers, whether he and his employer are satisfied according to their own subjective evaluation, or why they are not satisfied, what direction their wishes and aspirations are taking, for future development will depend upon these factors.' One year later in 1893 Weber was to conduct another survey of rural laborers on behalf of the Evangelical-Social Congress which was intended to fill in the missing information and to serve as a check for the results obtained by the Verein.

3. *The social surveys of religious organizations*

Up to 1890 in Germany, it was either the government or the Verein that conducted social surveys, and in both the professionally trained economist or census expert prevailed, without, however, bringing about any major refinement in survey techniques. The year 1890 marks a turning point both in German history and the history of empirical social research. Bismarck was retired by the young William II, the law banning socialist activities since 1878 was repealed, Germany and the rest of Europe departed more and more from the policies of economic liberalism as the stage was set for the economic

---

[12] For an English text of Weber's view of the land question delivered to an American audience at the St. Louis World's Fair in 1904, see [162, pp. 363-385]. Reinhard Bendix [9] in a recent book on Max Weber has pointed out the great impact of the young Weber's agricultural labor and stock exchange studies upon his later political and intellectual perspective. (See especially Chap. II in Bendix.)

and imperialist race between the European powers. Inside Germany the socialists were capturing a sizable and growing vote, and the idea of a Christian Social movement took shape from the side of reform minded clergymen with Friedrich Naumann at their head and with the avowed purpose of stopping the spread of religious skepticism among the fourth estate, while at the same time providing for it a political outlet. The religious organizations quickly realized that they knew preciously little about how a factory worker lived, thought, felt, and what he expected of the future apart from what was reported in the socialist press. It was at this point that some ministers turned to empirical social research to round out their own limited experiences based on a single parish. Curiously enough this tradition of empirical research on the part of religious groups and individuals never completely ceased even as a result of the War, and some interesting studies of the religious attitudes of working class youth were carried out in the 1920s.

It all started when a young theology student named Paul Göhre took it into his head to 'find out the whole truth about the mentality of the working classes, its material aspirations, its spiritual, moral and religious character.' He spent three full months in a machine tool factory, impersonating a young apprentice who had left the printing trade as a result of misunderstandings with his employers. The book based on his field notes – he wrote down his experiences of the day each night before going to bed – was published in 1891 under the title *Three Months as a Factory Worker* [52].[13] Göhre gave it the subtitle 'a practical study.' It was a remarkable field study and was indeed recognized as a major achievement by all those interested in creating a non-Marxist working class movement. His description (pp. 38 ff.) of the structural sources of the disintegration of the working class family, a result of the mother's employment, the lack of privacy in the crowded tenements, the impossibility of having even one common meal a day, the self-sufficiency of the older children, reveals an observant and sociologically mature mind at work. Although Göhre himself considered the high point of his revelations the chapters on culture and Christianity where he reported *verbatim* lengthy conversations and arguments with his fellow workers on religious topics, today it is the chapter on the social organization of work inside the

[13] An English translation was published in the U. S., *Three Months in a Workshop* (N. Y.: Scribner, 1895), with an introduction by professor Richard Ely of the University of Wisconsin.

factory [Chap. 3] which reads best. Among other things, Göhre contradicted the prevailing belief on the uniformity and isolation of workers at their machines. He described the solidarity binding workers of a team together so that a norm about the rhythm of work 'not too fast and not too slow' is reached through mutual understanding (p. 59). When a novice became accepted as a full member of the group, he would be seized and his mustache would be rubbed full of tar, a rather painful *rite de passage* (pp. 77-78). He noted the effectiveness of personal influence in the spread of socialist propaganda through daily conversations and discussions in the work-group (pp. 104-105). He also described in detail the internal stratification of the workers along skills and seniority, with the manner of clothing as its most visible status symbol (p. 76 ff.).[14]

As a result of his book Göhre became elected Secretary of the Evangelical Social Congress which had just been founded that year and which was headed by Naumann and Stöcker. The Congress had been patterned in its formal organization after the Verein für Sozialpolitik. It held an annual convention and was led by an executive committee that included some prominent Verein economists.[15] Max Weber, who at this time was torn between an academic and political

[14] Göhre soon found an imitator in the person of an active feminist intent on writing an expose of female factory work and breaking through the apathy of the ladies of her own class. Minna Wettstein-Adelt's *3-1/2 Months as a Factory Working-Woman* [171] turned out to be less penetrating and objective than Göhre's book. Her moralistic point of view transpired from italicized statements on every page, like (p. 41) 'whoever in these circles becomes indebted is lost without the possibility of escape.' She had a strong feminine bias. After she mentioned how ineffective priests were in their relations with the working class as compared to the nuns, she related (p. 70) an incident known to her 'with complete certainty.' The same girl who is in the habit of passing by the priory with her boyfriend, with the two of them laughing loudly and carrying on 'loose talk,' combs her hair simply and does not put any make-up on when a nun visits the house so as not to offend her. Another amusing incident (described again in all seriousness) occured during her tour of taverns, bars and dancehalls to observe moral standards first hand. In a tavern recommended to her as a pick-up place, she planted herself as bait with her husband at the nearest table, just in case. She was in fact approached, not by a workman or soldier, but a 'gentleman of her own class.' She then served notice to the ladies who might be reading the book that it is their husbands who are partly responsible for the moral degradation of the lower class (p. 85). Despite these awkward forms of her presentation, Wettstein-Adelt managed for the first time to give a first-hand account of such abuses as attempts by supervisors to pressure factory girls into becoming their mistresses and the tremendous burden of the working woman who had to become mother and housewife as she returned home exhausted.

[15] In its early years there was some overlap in the membership of the two organi-

career, was also a member of the Congress and became a life long friend and political adviser of Naumann. It is in the Congress that Weber got to know Göhre whom he was able to enlist for the idea of conducting a survey of agricultural laborers sponsored by the Congress that was to serve as a check on the Verein survey and was to round it out on the psychological side.[16]

Weber reviewed both the recent Verein survey and the earlier Goltz and Lengerke studies and came to the conclusion that 'all the surveys up to now have shown with a high probability that the problems presented by the condition of rural labor are principally of a psychological nature' [160, p. 535]. Weber actually hesitated between sending questionnaires to rural ministers or doctors, but decided upon the ministers because the Congress had a central register of all parish ministers and because they might be better suited to report on psychological problems. About 15,000 questionnaires were sent out to all parishes and about 1,000 of them were returned.

The questionnaire itself was not a radical departure from the 1891 Verein questionnaire. It was, however, far shorter, divided into meaningful units, and the questions more precise. Compare the following questions where the shift toward precision and concern with psychological factors is evident.

Verein, 1891. Questionnaire II, question 4
'The relations of employer to the workers. Do patriarchical relationships still prevail in the good meaning of the word, that is paternal caretaking on the one side, and loyal attachment on the other? Is discipline becoming looser? Breaks in contract. Do the landowners take into account the greater self-

consciousness of the workers, or do they miss the right tone in their dealings (with the workers)? What manner of punishment prevails?...'

Weber, 1893, Part IVb, question 3
'Are the relations between employer and employee patriarchical? That is caretaking on the one side and attachement on the other?

---

zations. Every effort was made by the Verein economists to keep the discussions and reports in the Congress at a scientifically acceptable level. Night courses in economics were given by some of the young Verein economists to the clergymen of the Congress for several years. For a history of the Congress in its formative years, see Eger [35, Chaps. 1-3].

[16] Unfortunately most of the literature on this survey is in periodicals, newspapers, or reports of the Evangelical-Social Congress which are not available in the U.S. The discussion will be based mainly on a six-page newspaper article written by Weber in 1893 [160]. The questionnaire is, however, reproduced in a study by Eugen Katz for Brentano's seminar in *Munch. Volks. St. 64* (1904).

What do the employees say about their employers, about officials of the estates and the foremen? What punishment is given in cases of poor performance, does corporal punishment occur? fines? deductions from wages?...'

Weber cut out a lot of questions on the forms of land-tenure and kept the section on the material and living conditions short. Instead he concentrated on social and occupational mobility, migratory labor, and the origin of the various peasant groups. In previous surveys there had been questions on whether or not a laborer might get ahead. Weber was interested in addition to the social changes and innovation that mobility and migratory labor might bring about: 'To what extent does emigration into foreign countries and movement into industrial regions take place? Single individuals or entire families? Are these the hard workers or the lazy ones? Are they changed in any way when they return and does the change have any effect upon the community?' Another innovation for this type of survey were a few questions trying to get at attitudes. After a series of questions on the living quarters of the laborers, Weber asks: 'Do the workers put any value at all upon the appearance of their tenements, and in what respect?' He also wanted to know the workers' attitudes toward non-traditional forms of work: 'What is the people's outlook toward work in side-occupations such as sugar factories.... What is their outlook toward the introduction of machines?' Weber did not, on the other hand, include questions on the hopes and aspirations of the laborers, or their satisfaction with their wages and general lot in life. Despite such novel questions Weber's questionnaire was mostly an extension of the standard form dealing with the material condition of the working classes.

The ministers' replies were superior to the answers the Verein had gotten from the landowners. 'A large part of the reports gives a detailed account on how the data was obtained...,' Weber wrote (p.540). 'These are systematic monographs that have an enduring value for cultural history.' Weber was no more able than his contemporaries to find a suitable mode of analysis for the reports he had received from all parts of Germany. On this matter he wrote in 1893, and his remarks might apply to all the surveys of this period (p. 540): '... nonetheless we face all this material as a puzzle, for we have not so far been able to find a way in which it is to be worked over. He who has not collaborated in such a venture cannot imagine the magnitude of such an undertaking. The authentic freshness of the accounts which the reader can enjoy in the original reports will mostly be lost'.[17]

The Evangelical-Social Congress did not have a monopoly on social surveys very long. In 1895 the General Conference of the German Associations for Morality decided under somewhat unusual circumstances to conduct a questionnaire survey on 'the morals of the protestant rural population' [3]. A Pastor Wagner had been called upon to fill in as a speaker on this topic in 1894, and after some thought decided he did not know anything about conditions outside his parish. He therefore put an advertisement into the journal of the Associations and asked to be sent data for his report, but got only fifteen replies. When the Conference took place in 1895, he managed to persuade Pastor Wittenberg of the Inner Mission to embark on a bigger venture. The result of all these activities was a questionnaire on sexual customs and morals sent to 14,000 Protestant ministers all over Germany.

The questionnaire (pp. 7-13) constructed by Wagner had a clear, logical structure. It was divided into three main parts. The first part consisted of questions on the existing state of morality. Some questions had a definitely Kinseyean flavor: 'Is premarital sexual intercourse the rule? With or without the intention to marry?' and 'Do extra-marital affairs occur? with the approval of the spouse?' are two examples. The second part 'Causes (of loose morals)' was further divided into three sections, neglect on the part of family and employer, neglect on the part of the school and the Church, neglect on the part of the police and legislation. Each section in turn was further split up into more concrete areas. For example negligence on the part of the family and the employer was split into (1) lack of supervision of children by the parents, (2) influence of the living quarters (lack of heating; boarders), (3) influence of the places of

---

[17] A few years later Weber conducted a seminar in Heidelberg in which students used the questionnaires for their dissertation, but these were entirely lacking in any novel mode of analysis. They followed the typical procedure of each student picking one province or region and writing a brief 50-page essay faithfully following the topics outlined in the questionnaire. No attempt was made to quantify the questions on social relations and intellectual needs through coding of answers or any other method. In 1899 Weber published the dissertations in one volume [170]. Unfortunately an 11-page introduction to the volume by Weber himself was not accessible to the author.

entertainment, (4) influence of the proximity of the sexes during work, (5) influence of the bad press and cheap literature.[18] The last part dealt with suggestions for the improvement of morality.

The difficulties with the questions were of the same order as those in the other surveys of this period. Apart from awkward phraseology they did not make clear on what information the answers should be based and failed to spell out the dimensions of the answer. Thus a question like 'Is the community church-minded and how does this become manifest?' invites answers that are not comparable. It would have been preferable to split it into a set of specific questions on rates of church attendance, contributions, religious instruction, etc., and and on the basis of these to build an index of community church-mindedness. The novelty of the survey was that it covered for the first time the entire area of sexual behavior, customs, and moral norms, as systematic social research. Unfortunately the manner of analysis of the approximately 900 replies[19] all but defeated the advantages of a questionnaire survey. Wagner and Wittenberg adopted the procedure of summarizing all the reports from one district into an essay, and then of publishing one such essay, district by district, until most of rural Germany was covered. In the 1,000 pages which the two volumes of the final report encompassed, only about five tables appeared. It is doubtful whether the existence of this survey ever became known outside of religious organizations, and even they seemed to have made no use of its results beyond incorporating striking details and quotes into speeches at religious conferences.

Another pastor, Max Rade, was led to improvise an entirely new mode of social research, the results of which he reported at the ninth annual convention of the Evangelical-Social Congress in 1898 under the title 'The religious-ethical world of thought of our industrial workers' [10]. Rade had been dissatisfied with the lack of knowledge

---

[18] This type of layout approaches in structure a present-day survey technique for the assessment of causes called an 'accounting scheme.' For further reference, see [81]. It is interesting that a minister should come closer to this technique than the Verein economists in their questions on the causes of usury. Perhaps this is no cause for surprise since sin and the circumstances under which it occurs has been one of most highly categorized areas of human behavior through its central importance to all religions.

[19] Surveys were so common by this time that one respondent wrote (p. 18), 'with all the endless circulars and surveys which plague us it is no small task to fill out such a complicated questionnaire.'

on this subject and was unwilling to rely on statements about it in the socialist press. After some years of correspondence with workers who sent him letters and poems on many topics (p. 68), Rade hit upon the idea of sending a short questionnaire to 48 workers, half of them socialists and the other half 'moderates' and 'god-fearing' (p. 89). The questionnaire itself was made up of a dozen questions: 'What is your opinion – serious, open, honest and straightforward – towards...' and then followed a dozen items such as the Bible, Christ, Luther and the Reformation, God, the Creation, miracles, life after death, the value of sermons, marriage and family life, and Christian charity. The last item only was not of a strictly religious nature: 'What is in your opinion a conscientious individual? What attributes must he possess?'

Rade's report on his little study was received with great enthusiasm. He numbered his respondents from 1 to 48, and after first reading one agnostic worker's answers in their entirety, he ran down the items of his questionnaire, reading 10 answers from believers and then the same number from non-believers, juxtaposed for purposes of comparison and effect. This was the simplest way of presenting the material and an especially dramatic one for the occasion. The next step in a scientific analysis would have been to code the content of the answers, to make quantitative comparisons question by question, and to proceed to some sort of typology of religious beliefs, but these techniques were unknown at the time. The novelty of Rade's undertaking was that he actually went directly to the workers to ask questions about their attitudes. He also intuitively approached an experimental design in that he matched the socialist group with a politically 'moderate' control group. These developments, however, escaped notice at the time.[20]

Two studies of religious beliefs and attitudes carried out after the war need also be mentioned at this point because they illustrate a continuity in research and because the researchers did attempt to

[20] I have found no evidence in Erdman [43] and other books that the Catholic religious associations, especially the biggest one of them, the 'Verein für das katholische Deutschland,' engaged in social surveys similar to those of the Protestant associations. The Volksverein did engage in many educational and propagandistic activities, and its charter did state as one of its aims [43, p. 160] 'the collection of scientific and practical data.' The relationship of the Catholic organizations to social research is one of the points at which further research is required and might well prove fruitful.

construct typologies of religious belief.[21] The first of these, Paul Piechowski's study entitled *Proletarian Beliefs* [106], was inspired and influenced by Rade, as can be seen by comparing question #10: 'What is your attitude toward the Bible, and what of its contents has especially been retained in your memory?'—with a similar one in Rade to whom he refers in the introduction. Piechowski's thinking was more sociologically oriented in that he also included questions on the communications aspect of attitudes, such as #16: 'Do you discuss religious topics within your family, and in what sense?' He also asked the workers whether they belonged to trade-union, political, and religious associations. Piechowski had a problem of analysis similar to Rade's, except that he had 500 replies on his hand compared to 48. Unfortunately he was not able to liberate himself from Rade's frame of analysis. From their answers to a question on church membership, Piechowski classified each worker as either a 'Church Member' or a 'Dissident'. Within these two groups he made further distinctions. There were four types of 'Dissidents': (1) radical rejection, (2) moderate voices, (3) former Catholics, (4) anarchists. By inspection of the protocols he cited as examples for each type, it is evident that Piechowski's typology does have quite incongruous elements mixed together, such as religious conviction, political ideology, tone and outspokenness of the answers, etc. Today the researcher would probably build a separate index for each of those dimensions, and by cross-classifying individuals on the indices, construct some overall typology of *Weltanschauung*. For Piechowski this difficult task remained an intuitive process. Later in the book when he analyzed the answers to each question separately, he fell back upon Rade's method of picking some 'Dissidents' and 'Church Members' and confronting their answers so that they might speak for themselves.

An effort similar in intent to Piechowski's by another team of researchers is described in Günther Dehn, *Proletarian Youth* [32]. Dehn adopted the novel method of projective questions developed by his

---

[21] The concern with the religious beliefs of the working class and of youth brought with it a proliferation of empirial studies after the war. These developments are beyond the scope of this dissertation, but should be included as one of the main trends of post-war social research and the rise of social psychology. From the pre-1914 period an interesting book by the pastor Ilgenstein, *The World of Religious Beliefs of the Social Democrats* [70], which was based entirely on documentary evidence, should be singled out.

collaborator Ernst Lau, a Berlin psychologist. Part II of the book
was entitled 'The Religious State of Mind of Youth' and started with
a brief description of the methods used. Dehn and Lau visited many
schools in the year of 1920-21, presented the children with little
cards on which three words were written, such as 'God, Help, Death,'
'God, Freedom, Fatherland,' and then told them (p. 160) 'write
down whatever occurs to you. The essay will not be censured, nor
will it go on your record.' Alternatively they also had the children
write essays on such topics as 'my thoughts on God and religion.'
In this way they obtained some 3,000 written reports on the basis
of which five types of religious orientations were derived, again by an
intuitive approach.

III. *Statistics and sociology*

At the beginning of the 19th century statistics still referred to a field of study that was a mixture of geography, political science, history, and public administration. Its most famous representative had been Gottfried Achenwall of Göttingen. Before the creation of government statistical agencies, it was private individuals, especially those in the professions and in particular the medical profession, who had assembled and published vital statistics, crime statistics and demographic data, sometimes as an intellectual passtime but more often out of a sense of social responsibility. The leading position in the history of social research in Europe during the first half of the century belongs without a doubt to the medical profession. More than any other group it was responsible for pioneering studies of slum dwellings, sanitary conditions, factory work, nutrition, prisons, mental institutions, infant mortality, occupational diseases and accidents, and many other matters having to do with the well-being of the population. It is their relentless efforts which provided the initial data for social reform and legislation at a time when the industrial revolution and rapid urbanization were transforming European society in radical fashion. In the end the sanitary reformers succeeded in convincing the governments of the need for exact demographic and social data and the governments in turn created statistical agencies which assumed the burden of collecting and publishing them.

In Germany a bitter controversy developed between the numerical and the descriptive statisticians about the nature of their science.[1] It was as much a rivalry between two groups for the control of academic positions as it was a detached scientific controversy. In an influential 1850 monograph Carl Knies [76] succeeded in having the term *Staats-*

[1] Lazarsfeld [82] has recently traced the history of the two traditions of statistics back to the British political arithmeticians on the one hand and to the German cameralists on the other. He has also documented the rivalry between the two traditions as it came to a climax in the period just prior to 1848.

wissenschaften established for political science. At about this time a three way division of intellectual labor became more or less permanent: political science and public administration succeeded in dominating university teaching; the statisticians monopolized the statistical agencies and census bureaus of the German states and cities; finally political economy, called *Volkswirtschaftlehre* and later also *Nationaloekonomie*, became recognized as an academic discipline, and did in fact represent a compromise since it adopted both historical, descriptive, and statistical methods.

1. *Rudolf Virchow and medical reform*

In his book *A History of Public Health* [115], George Rosen has written a comprehensive account of the European sanitary reform movement. It originated with the public hygienists in France and spread first to England in the 1830s and later during the revolutionary ferment of 1848 into Germany where it became known as medical reform and was identified in particular with the activities of the famous pathologist Rudolf Virchow. The public hygienists received a strong justification from the dominant social philosophy of the time which was imbued with the spirit of the Enlightenment. In a famous sentence that expressed the essence of this spirit Cabanis stated that '*les maladies dépendent des erreurs de la société.*' In this conception, physical health was inseperable from a healthy social order. It must also be remembered that in the early 19th century the accepted medical theory of the origin and spread of diseases was anti-contagionist. Disease was thought to be caused by the state of the atmosphere. Poor sanitary conditions in particular produced a foul local air conducive to disease. Backed by these ideas physicians engaged directly in social research for a scientific description of social ills such as slum conditions and infant mortality had to precede the diagnosis of society and the social reform remedies that would be applied as a cure. As an illustration of the extent to which physicians engaged in social research, one well-known example might be mentioned: when Friedrich Engels wrote in 1845 *On the Condition of the Working Classes in England* [42], the data he relied upon for the most part had been made available by the research of physicians such as Alison, Corrigan, Davidson, and Kay.

The ideas of the French public hygienists became the foundation of the German medical reform movement which was started during the 1848 revolution by a group of enthusiastic young physicians including Salomon Neumann, Rudolf Virchow and Rudolf Leubuscher. The basic idea behind medical reform was that the health of the population was a matter of direct social concern, that social and economic conditions have an important effect on health and disease, and that consequently disease could only be eliminated by reforming the social and economic conditions which produce it [115, pp. 254-8]. The revolutionary implications of this philosophy are clearly spelled out in some of the slogans that Virchow coined [2, pp. 44, 46]: 'The physicians are the natural attorneys of the poor, and social problems should largely be solved by them,' and 'If medicine is to fulfil her great task, then she must enter political and social life.'

The medical historian Ackerknecht has written an authoritative biography of Virchow entitled *Rudolf Virchow: Doctor, Statesman, Anthropologist* [2]. As can be inferred from the title, Virchow was one of those rare men who during their lifetime achieve eminence in several fields. He also engaged intermittently in activities which had to do with medical statistics and social research. He participated in international medical and statistical congresses, he was acquainted with the work of Quetelet and the sociological publications of the British and French sanitary reformers. In connection with his activities for sanitary reform such as providing a sewerage system for the city of Berlin he stressed the need for precise vital and medical statistics. Both he and his friend Salomon Neumann wrote statistical monographs on morbidity and mortality. Typical findings from these studies would show that there was a positive relationship between poverty and both adult and infant mortality in Berlin [153, p. 173]. Virchow would rank order the districts of Berlin by the average per capita tax paid and by the mortality rate in order to point up any 'parallelism' between the two variables. His two most impressive accomplishments in social research were however his report on a typhus epidemic and his survey of German schoolchildren.

In February and March 1848 the Prussian medical authorities sent Virchow to survey the medical situation in Upper Silesia where a thyphus epidemic had broken out during a period of famine. His report [153], originally published in a medical journal, went far beyond an account of the course of the epidemic, the case histories of patients, and the description of the illness itself. After presenting a brief history of the region, its geographical and climatic characteristics, Virchow wrote a penetrating analysis (pp. 220-6) of the economic and cultural backwardness of Upper Silesia, which he repeatedly compared to Ireland. His mode of analysis is quite similar to the type of approach that social scientists use today when describing an underdeveloped country. Virchow singled out four primary causes of the backwardness syndrome. First, after centuries of German hegemony, the Polish language was still spoken by the peasants, and the resulting barrier to communication had cut off the inhabitants from the influence of German culture. Second, the Catholic Church was still the unchallenged authority in religious matters, education, and social policy, and despite the help it provided on occasion to alleviate hunger and care for the sick, it had kept the people in ignorance and superstition. The bureaucracy too had not lifted a finger to improve social and economic life, although it might have encouraged the revival of old industries and the introduction of new ones. Finally the absentee landlord who lived off land rents spent their income outside the region and thus drained off all capital for investment. The legendary 'uncleanliness, laziness, and indifference' of the population was not then a peculiarity of the Polish national character, but a result of social conditions that left the people without hope and with no goal to work for: 'Prosperity, education, and freedom are mutually reinforcing, and so is hunger, ignorance, and bondage.' His recommendations to prevent a future outbreak of the epidemic (pp. 321 ff.) consisted of a radical program of social reform and social change in the spirit of 1848: replace clerical education by secular education based on a positive study of nature; abolish bondage and feudal rights and privileges in favor of self government and tax reform; introduce new industries, create an 'association of the propertyless' in order to prevent the workers from becoming mere machines. It is characteristic of Virchow that he backed up his words with deeds. One week after his return to Berlin the revolution broke out on March 18, he participated in the streetfighting and was elected in October to the Democratic Congress in Berlin [2, p. 15].

The second project that Virchow undertook was related to his interest in physical anthropology which in the 1870s became his main field of research. Ackerknecht has described the circumstances under which the gigantic survey of German schoolchildren originated [2, pp. 209 ff]. After the war of 1870-71, the Frenchman Armand de Quatrefegas maintained that the Prussians were descendant from a dark Finno-Mongoloid race and thus racially different from the rest of the German people. Quatrefegas accused these dark Prussians of being the perpetrators of 'war crimes' such as the bombardment of Paris. In the ensuing controversy Virchow decided to put these racial arguments to an empirical test. He enlisted the support of the German Anthropological Society in 1876 for the survey of school-children. During the survey the public school teachers recorded the color of the eyes, the hair, and the skin of about 6,760,000, pupils. The findings which became available over the next decade exploded the myth of a predominantly blond and pure German race. 31.8% of the children surveyed were 'blond' (all three traits light), whereas 54.15% showed a mixture of light and dark traits and 14.05% were true 'browns' (all three traits dark). Virchow also demonstrated that even though Jewish children were darker on the average than the rest of the Germans, still 11.17% were 'blond'. These findings did not endear him to the anti-semites and the social theorists who traced national and cultural differences back to racial differences and the purity of races. Virchow's conclusion was clear [2, p. 214]: 'We know that every nationality, take for instance the German or Slavonic, is of a composite character and no one can say, on the spur of the moment, from what original stock either may have been developed.'

In the 1870s and 1880s, social research by physicians in the tradition of the medical reform movement decreased sharply. The disease rather than the patient and his social environment became the main concern of the medical profession [116, p. 709]. Several trends account for this change. The bacteriological discoveries of Pasteur, Koch and others gave strong support to the contagionist theory of the spread of disease. The origins of deseases were traced to viruses and other micro-organisms rather than to the social environment. Furthermore the programme of the medical reformers was realised when the German cities adopted sanitary reforms and public health regulations. On a national scale Bismarck's social insurance legislation was put into effect. After 1900 there was a revival of social medicine centering on the efforts of Alfred Grotjahn. Grotjahn had attended Schmoller's seminar in Berlin in 1901-02 and had become a Social Democrat while in medical school. He edited with the help of Kriegel an annual review of social hygiene and social statistics [56], and published in

1915 a book on social pathology [55]. Other studies on the sociology of illness were published in a work edited by Mosse and Tugenrich [100].[2]

2. *Engel's budget law*

From the economist's point of view, statistical data needed interpretation in terms of economic theory and concepts, and that was to be done by searching for the relationship between time series. In a speech delivered in 1866, Bruno Hildebrand, one of the founders of the German historical school of economics,[3] gave an appropriate illustration [65, p. 8]: If the population decreases, examine the birth, death and migration figures; if the latter two show no change, but there is a drop in birth rates, then compare this time series with that of food prices, and if 'these (prices) rise correspondingly as the birth rate falls, then one arrives to the conclusion that the decreasing population was a result of high food prices, a result of material hardship.' Hildebrand criticized the German followers of Quetelet who were searching for constancies in rates and averages and calling them 'laws', rather than searching for causes by examining the relationships between variables. It was however a German follower of Quetelet who made an outstanding contribution to empirical and quantitative methods in social research.

Ernst Engel came of a modest background and was trained as a

---

[2]   Unfortunately I did not have access to these publications directly. An outline of the development of social medicine after 1900 can be found in Rosen's article [116].

[3]   It is surprising to what extent the founders of the historical school of economics had some sort of a statistical or mathematical background. Hildebrand himself had been head of the statistical bureau of Thüringen before assuming an academic post. Both Knies and Engel were professional statisticians. Only Roscher had a purely historical training. Of the generation born in the late 1830s, Lexis had studied mathematics, Conrad natural science, Schönberg had been in a statistical seminar, Wagner and Schmoller both wrote a book on moral statistics and demography in their career. The generation of the forties was taught statistics in the Berlin seminar of Ernst Engel: Knapp, Brentano, Schnapper-Arndt (and somewhat later Tönnies) all went through it. Knapp in addition headed the Leipzig statistical agency before teaching at Strassburg. Others of this generation of economists also were active statisticians early in their career. Bücher for example had been in charge of the Basel city statistical bureau; Inama-Sternegg organized the Austrian government's statistical apparatus.

mining engineer. In this capacity he met Le Play with whom, as a young man, he took field trips in 1847-48 during which he was very impressed with Le Play's great gift for precise observation [41, p. 27]. Later as a professional statistician he also came to know Adolphe Quetelet, and his budget law of 1857 showed the influence of both great men. Engel eventually rose to become head of the Prussian (after 1871, German) Statistical Bureau. In Berlin starting in 1862 he conducted for years a statistical seminar which many of the promising young economists attended. Engel was also a founding member of the Verein für Sozialpolitik in 1872, and already years before that had worked on a plan for the improvement of the lot of the working classes through profit sharing [23, p. 71].

On the basis of resolutions passed at the First International Congress of Statistics in 1853 presided over by Quetelet, budgets of workers were made the topic of an investigation. Agreement on an extensive list of expenditures and a typology of working class families was reached. A family would be classified as 'indigent' if it had to be sustained in part from public charity, as 'of modest means' if it was poor but not taking charity, and if it was in no way dependent upon outside sources for its existence it would be called a 'family of means'. As a direct outcome of these discussions, 199 Belgian working class budgets were published by Quetelet's assistant Ducpétiaux in 1855, and by coincidence this was also the year that Le Play published his *Ouvriers Européens* containing 36 family monographs including detailed budgets. Engel was fascinated by the budget data in both publications and disappointed that neither Ducpétiaux nor Le Play had analyzed their data in search of some underlying regularities. In a monograph which also dealt with production, consumption and population theory from a theoretical angle [40], Engel undertook this task. From the expenditure lists collected by Ducpétiaux, Engel was able to construct a budget for each of the 199 families according to Le Play's superior budget classification, and by means of the family monographs he was able to classify the Le Play families according to Quetelet's and Ducpétiaux's typology of working class families.

By examining the data Engel noted that regardless of the type of family, there existed the same priority of needs, namely nourishment, clothing, shelter, heat and light, etc. (he actually had five more categories but among them they accounted for less than 10% of a working class budget). Furthermore the poorer a family, the higher proportion of its budget was spent on food. Engel even tried to quantify this law by fitting budget data from his own investigations as head of the Statistical Burea of Saxony with the curve of a geometric progression (% spent on food $= ar^n$), and he actually presented in a table the expected percent of income spent on food for family incomes ranging from 200 Mark to 3000 Mark by 100 Mark increments, without however indicating how well the expected values computed from the formula fitted the actual data. Engel further suggested that his law and his expected values of the consumption items in each income group might permit families to be characterized by numerical indices according to their deviation from these averages (pp. 170-171): 'The above figures are of considerable value for science, because they are suited to characterize more accurately the notions of avarice, economy, thrift, extravagance, luxury and wastefulness. For example, avarice is the unmotivated or not adequately motivated... greater curtailment of consumption in all or single categories of expenditures, than the average consumption at a given level of income.' This conceptualization was very similar to Quetelet's notion of 'disposition to crime,' only here it was applied to the family collectively, and there was a direct, numerical method suggested for its measure [82, pp. 305-309].

According to Schumpeter [129. p. 961], no one at the time recognized the importance of Engel's budget law for economic theory, nor did it become the starting point for empirical investigations of other aspects of the family.[4] Engel later introduced the account-book method of gathering family budgets, which consisted of distributing to the families elaborately pre-coded and dated booklets for the purpose of recording

---

[4] Despite his Berlin statistical seminar for the benefit of future social scientists, Engel's impact upon subsequent social research was confined to awakening the enthusiasm of single individuals like Schnapper-Arndt and Tönnies, and not in fostering a research movement. Brentano, one of Engel's most promising students in 1866-67, whom Engel took on a trip to England which was decisive for Brentano's later interests and career, recalled Engel as a poor teacher who was unable to awaken in his students his own enthusiasm for Le Play [23, pp. 41-44]. Engel would put a copy of *Ouvriers Européens* on the seminar table and call Le Play 'the father of the descriptive social-scientific monograph.' The students remained skeptical. 'We wanted to study national economy, not private households,' is how Brentano recalled the seminar's reaction [24, p. 208]. According to Bücher [26, p. 700] no one later worked up and analyzed the hundreds of budgets that Engel had accumulated for a future publication at the time of his death. Engel, however, inspired Carrol Wright's budget studies of 1876 in Massachusetts [41, p. 29]. Wright intended to check whether Engel's budget law would hold up in the different environment of the New World.

all their expenses over several months, rather than relying on averages and approximations based on on-the-spot investigations or oral testimony. A year before his death in 1895, Engel, now retired and free to pursue his own interests, once more came back to budgets [41], but this book represented primarily a consolidation of his earlier work in the light of more recent, precise and abundant data. It contained, however, a useful history of budget studies up to that time.

3. *Moral statistics*

Another broad area in which an abundance of data became available was demography, criminology and anthropometry, because censuses were now conducted and violations of the law were recorded and assembled systematically, and the same was true for the body measurements of army draftees. This area came to be known as 'Moral Statistics' following Guerry's and Quetelet's use of the term. Before the 1860s, Quetelet's work in moral statistics was known to only a limited number of people in Germany. It was through Buckle's *History of English Civilization*, whose German translation ran through five quick editions starting in 1864, that Quetelet's ideas were popularized (as well as misrepresented) to a wider German public [72, p. 362]. Thereupon moral statistics became the fashionable new science of the day. It also became immediately embroiled in the philosophical dispute about free will with a variety of academic disciplines participating: philosophers, historians, political economists, mathematicians, and theologians. Quetelet had called 'Laws' the observed constancy in time of suicide rates, marriage rates, crime rates, etc., in a population or stratum of the population. Quetelet had also written about a 'disposition to crime' in the population for which he postulated a normal distribution in analogy with the observed normal distribution of the height of army draftees [82, pp. 294-311]. While the philosophical disputes which Quetelet's ideas and terminology started will not be reviewed here, it is interesting to examine in detail some of the procedures and data that actually went under the name of moral statistics, for they will illustrate the discontinuities in the history of quantification in sociology.

Adolph Wagner in his early academic career was involved in moral statistics. In 1864 he published a pair of short studies under the title

The Regularity of Seemingly Chance Actions from the Point of View of Statistics [156]. Still under the complete influence of Quetelet, Wagner saw regularities and constancies of rates in table after table where the figures clearly indicated a trend or wide oscillations. Of course in the absence of any statistical tests such pursuit of an *idée fixe* was relatively easy. Part of the book was a 'comparative suicide statistics of Europe' which contained an exhaustive analysis of suicide rates, starting with the influence of the weather and temperature, to a comparison of religious strata, age cohorts, occupational and professional groups, married and unmarried statuses, in short almost all of the factors which Durkheim included in his famous investigation *Le Suicide*. If the resulting picture that emerged was nonetheless chaotic as Wagner proceeded from one 'explanation' to the next, it was because Wagner had no coherent theory about social groups and society which the variations in suicide rates were meant to test and illustrate (precisely that which enabled Durkheim to differentiate between types of suicide and look for differences in rates along a systematic set of ideas). Lack of theory and a resulting improvisation and arbitrariness were in many ways the great flaw which rendered so much of moral statistics scientifically sterile.

Wagner entertained, on the other hand, fascinating notions on quantification at a time when attribute and rank order statistics did not exist yet. At one extreme (p. 56), 'in the physical actions of men, qualitative relationships lend themselves easily to statistical analysis, insofar as they in turn can be related back to quantitative relationships. For example, a statistical account of births can be related to the weight, height... of the newborn.' At the other extreme, 'the qualitative description of moral actions will always remain the most difficult, not only because people do not report their motives, but because they are so seldom conscious of them.' In between was the 'statistics of intellectual performances' where Wagner thought great advances might be made. In a footnote (pp. 59-61) he gave a detailed example of what he meant. For a number of years the high schools of Bavaria had kept a complete record of each student's marks in all subjects including discipline and diligence, his rank order in his class, as well as information about his family such as religion, occupation of father, and social status. He described how in some topics, such as Greek and Latin, the teachers were in the habit of grading according to the number of orthographic, grammatical and stylistic errors, so that 'the subjective judgment of the teachers is on the whole limited' and the grades therefore comparable. In order to analyze this data, Wagner proposed that all school subjects could be reduced to four basic mental abilities: numerical ability (mathematics), linguistic abilities (all languages), memory (geography and history) and lastly general talent (German composition), and that the interrelation of these four mental abilities be studied in great detail, as well as the influence of religion, family status, and age on each type of ability separately. Furthermore the problem of the early versus, the late bloomers might also be studied quantitatively through this data and even the hotly debated question whether or not the rank order of standing in the school was related to a subsequent rank order of success and achievement in later life. Each one of these problems has, of course, since been taken up and vastly extended. Educational Testing Service has been studying now for a long time the relationship between success in school and achievement in later life. The sociology of education is just now very concerned with the problem of the early and late bloomers and its relationship to the grading system. And Spearman in 1904 was led to the discovery of factor analysis by examinig the correlation matrix of grades of high school students, which is very similar to Wagner's outline of the relationship between the four mental abilities, only that Wagner suggested an *a priori* reduction of the school subjects into four categories – 'factors' in the newer terminology – whereas this reduction is performed by a procedure of statistical fitting in factor analysis. But there were obstacles in Wagner's way which he was unable to overcome (p. 61): 'But this analysis of the statistical data, which is by far more interesting than our usual statistical investigation of the number of teachers and pupils, presupposes vast energies for work available at best to a statistical bureau. Nonetheless I intended to focus attention on these important matters once and for all.' Wagner's statement highlights the predicament of investigators in this area: utter dependence on the government statistical agencies for the data and for the form in which it was available, and, in the absence of statistical techniques of sampling and machine processing of data, a mountain of work facing the lone scholar.[5] Wagner himself soon abandoned the field

[5] The same difficulties led Conrad to abandon his moral statistical investigations which he had carried out with the help of his seminar students. In an 1877 monograph entitled 'Contributions to the investigation of the influence of the standard of living

of moral statistics in favor of political economy. He became a leading *Kathedersozialist*, the leader of the political left in the Verein für Sozialpolitik, and taught for many years at the University of Berlin.

Of much more substance than Wagner's occasional flashes of insight in an otherwise quite conventional and descriptive treatment of statistical data was the 1877 monograph of Wilhelm Lexis, *The Theory of Mass Behavior* [89]. He was a creative mathematical mind, co-editor of the *Handbuch der Staatswissenschaften*, and a founding member of the Verein für Sozialpolitik. Lexis introduced in this work the notion of mathematical models of mass behavior which has only very recently reappeared in sociology. As an example of mass behavior Lexis described (pp. 2-3) a situation in which all German bankers would sell gold on the Paris exchange if the rate of exchange there were to reach a certain level. One needs to know the motives that drive individuals to action, which in the case of the bankers is assumed to be self-interest, and the economic variables and relationships which describe the situation in which the motives operate. Then the flight of gold, the mass behavior, is the sum of the actions of the separate bankers. 'Statistics gives us numerical criteria for judging the degree to which real-life economic mass actions correspond to their abstract types' – we would say how well the model fits – 'as well as (numerical criteria) for judging correctly the magnitude of deviation of the observed values from those based on the theoretical assumptions.' But even in a clearcut case not *all* bankers will sell gold in Paris. First, human action can in most cases be formulated only in probabilistic terms (p. 7) 'because of the inexhaustible richness of human life.' Second, human actions are seldom independent of each other (p. 10); there is a normative interrelation between society and its members, for the sentiments behind an individual act become part of the moral climate of society, which then in turn reacts back on other

---

and occupation upon mortality rates' [29], he made a detailed study of migration and the causes of death examined separately by social class and occupational stratum in the city of Halle between 1868 and 1871. In the introduction he drew attention to the lack of funds for the continuation of this line of work, called for the creation of a research institute affiliated with the university and wrote: 'We are not able at the present to continue these researches or similar expensive undertakings. We hope that the time is not far away when such an institute will be considered just as important for the university as a tropical green-house, and just as necessary for the province as a chemical experiment station, while both of these require greater upkeeping costs than we have planned (for our institute).'

individual sentiments. Lexis set himself the task of exploring which kinds of mass behavior fit the model of a game of chance such as coin tossing, where a complex set of physical factors, independent of each other but subject to random influences, will yield a normal distribution of means or proportions in the limit. Distributions which fit this model Lexis called 'typical series'. The numerical criterion he developed (p. 28) as a test of normalcy[6] was a measure of dispersion similar to the standard deviation except for constant factors. If the dispersion of the observed distribution was less than that of the corresponding binomial distribution (that is the dispersion expected if the model of a game of chance should fit the situation), then there must be some unknown interdependence among the factors that generated the distribution (pp. 22-23).

Lexis was, however, very cautious with the applicability of his criterion of fit to data on social behavior. He noted that in the area of conscious and purposive action one may often observe certain constant results which are the result of a rather trivial and obvious inter-dependence of factors. If for an industrial process materials A and B are needed in the ratio of 2:1 and have to be imported, then even if material B is imported in excess of this ratio during the first half of the year, it is not surprising that at year's end the ratio will again be close to 2:1 as in other years, for each importer places the size of his orders with an eye to arriving at that ratio (p. 12). Furthermore in time series which showed a trend, periodic oscillations, or the clear influence of other variables, called 'symptomatic series' because they express in numerical symptoms a more or less changeable state of society, it would be senseless to postulate a model of games of chance appropriate only for 'typical series'. Whereas Quetelet and his followers regarded the normal distribution and thus 'typical series' as the rule rather than the exception, Lexis tested many series and came to the conclusion that most social actions have rather the characteristics of symptomatic series (p. 91): 'The interconnection of human affairs tends in its very nature to produce mostly changes in a specific direction.' The only series which did stand up to his test of normalcy was that of the sex-ratio at birth, but that is a result of factors which are closest to the purely biological and physical side of human life. An interesting example of a symptomatic series discussed

[6] The Chi-square distribution and test of significance was invented by Pearson in 1900. This is the most convenient test of normalcy that one would use today.

at length (pp. 87-89) was that of the proportion of jury trials which ended with the verdict of innocent in France in the years 1825 to 1868. Lexis was able to show that the direct influence of such events as the revolutions of 1830 and 1848, and changes in the law affecting jury trials, produced wide jumps in the proportion.[7] Despite his ideas on models of mass behavior, Lexis did not develop any in the specific sense of describing algebraically or analytically the behavior of the German bankers and the flight of gold, for example. Furthermore he remained noncommittal about the applicability of probability notions to the symptomatic series. He stated that such application was formally possible, but little would be gained since the probabilities were changing in time according to laws unknown or at best surmised (p. 91). Lexis thus did not tap the whole field of conditional and transition probabilities which are proving so useful in present day model building.

Soon the controversies surrounding moral statistics died out. The Kantian notion of the distinctness of the realm of moral judgment from that of the material world, so deeply ingrained in the intellectual tradi-tion of Germany, prevailed over the intrusion of foreign ideas about social determinism in moral actions.[8] Another factor was the data which had been accumulated since the time of Quetelet, and which indicated that suicide and crime rates had not remained constant, but had increased during the century. Thus Quetelet's constant rates had rested on too short a run of years, and there was really nothing

---

[7] This topic had in the early days of probability theory occupied some of the best minds in the field, including Laplace, Fourier and Poisson, and the attempt to set up models of jury decisions resulting from probabilistic actions of a small group has been traced back to Condorcet. See Czuber [31, sec. 5].

[8] An example of the predominantly negative critique of Quetelet in Germany was the 1869 article by Gustav Schmoller on moral statistics [119]. While he presented an interesting discussion of Quetelet's notions of 'disposition' and the 'average man,' his main concern (p. 185) was whether the constant rates discovered by the moral statisticians implied that the materialist philosophy of tracing all phenomena back to physical causes was correct. The influence of idealist philosophy upon his thinking in these matters was illustrated in the following statement (p. 187): 'The laws governing mechanical processes are in no way applicable to the world of thoughts and mental representations. We observe in nature for example how two opposite forces check each other or how a resulting movement in a third direction takes place; something similar we can never say about out mental representations. The result of a series of conflicting motives in our inner self has no analogy in physical life.' Schmoller characteristically concluded his article with the statement that 'the notion and the essence of individuality have been saved from a statistical and leveling determinism.'

to debate any more [72, pp. 363 ff.]. Still another factor was a shift of interest from moral actions to anthropometry and physical anthropology which corresponded to the spread of social darwinism. Crime and suicide were viewed as pathological actions to be accounted for by the processes of inheritance and degeneration, the proof of which consisted in comparisons of cranial measurements between criminal and normal human types. It is unfortunate that it was Quetelet's ideas about social determinism rather than his ideas on quantification and his methods that had a greater impact in Germany. Lexis remained almost alone to push further in the mathematical direction, but only for a time, because a loss of creativity overtook him in the middle of his life [129, p. 852]. Wagner and Lexis thus did not sustain a tradition inspired by Quetelet. Thirty years later Tönnies tried to revive this line of investigation during his lifelong work with moral and social statistical data.

4. *Tönnies, social statistics, and sociography*

At the turn of the century, the heir to moral statistics was George von Mayr. He published his three-volume magnum opus *Statistics and the Theory of Society* [98] from 1895 to 1917. Even a cursory examination shows that with Mayr, both Lexis' imaginative mathematical treatment of data and the interest in quantifying and exploring further areas of social life which was still alive in Wagner, had given way for a monumental accumulation of rows and columns of numbers which took literally over 1,000 pages to record and were confined exclusively to the officially available statistics on population, crime, suicide and the like. Mayr's attitude was characterized as follows [I, p. 17]: 'The symptomatic phenomena especially, which make up the observational material of moral statistics, are often of a discretionary nature into which penetration through statistical observation is excluded: the individual forms of marital life, the social relationships between parents and their children in the domestic setting, etc..., the facts of overindulgence as well as of austerity that are without a doubt highly important for moral evaluation... remain in general outside the observational realm of statistics... Only exceptionally can moral-statistical observation capture some excesses as when violations of the criminal code, punishable drunkenness, or lack of conjugal support have occured.' The first volume entitled *Theoretical Statistics* contained not one single mathematical formula and was instead a pedantic handbook on how to gather facts by means of a census, to code and tabulate the answers, to organize the work force used for these tasks. Even the number of tons of paper used up in past censuses is listed because of the great storage problem it presented (p. 5). Questionnaire surveys, other than the census-type which he described at length, Mayr dismissed briefly because two 'subjective' elements are always present in them, namely the choice of the respondent, and the fact that they are restricted to collecting opinions rather than the hard facts he had in mind (p. 8).

Tönnies revolted against this narrow conception of empirical observation and data and for a number of years carried on a feud with Mayr because of it. 'What Mayr presents and elaborates as moral statistics must in fact be regarded as a scientific exposition of how to collect data, but not as science. The same holds for his 'statistics', wrote Tönnies [148, p. 125]. And further (p. 123): 'Here is being excluded from moral statistics: 1. everything which is not statistically graspable, that means in Mayr and in the newer terminology, everything not consisting of numbers or measurable elements; 2. (everything) which cannot be subjected for 'external reasons' to statistical observation, or at least is in fact not being observed statistically. But in this category belong most positive moral actions.'

Against Mayr's notion of statistics Tönnies pitted his own, richer notion of empirical sociology: sociography.[9] Sociography was to be that part of sociology which is based on inductive methods and empirical data, and was to include all relevant social phenomena whether or not they were expressed in numbers in the files of the statistical bureaus. In addition to statistical data, surveys, estimation, and typical single observations were to be sources of raw empirical data [148, p. 131]. The ultimate goal of sociography, or for that matter of any inductive science, was the 'progress from qualitative

[9] The word 'sociography' was actually borrowed from the Dutchman Steinmetz. Had the term 'statistics' not been at this time the monopoly of those engaged in gathering census data, Tönnies would have preferred it. The reason for it was that in the early 19th century 'statistics' still meant the concrete description of a country, its people, customs, climate, political system. Tönnies never failed to point out that his concept of sociography contained elements of the older statistics, and that he hoped it would in fact become a synthesis of the older, qualitative and the more recent, quantitative trend in statistics [148, p. 116].

to quantitative relationships,' was to arrive at laws by the process of induction performed on systematically gathered data [150, p. 555]. Tönnies described the importance of empirical social research in no uncertain words [150, p. 556]: 'As for myself, I admit openly that although I have become known for my work in (theoretical) sociology rather than my work in sociography, I consider one as important as the other...'

Given the importance which Tönnies attached to empirical sociology and his own numerous sociographic and moral statistical monographs on crime, suicide and other topics, which he consistently and laboriously pursued for the better part of 40 years, it will be necessary to examine his achievements in this area in great detail in order to find out why, in spite of all these efforts, he failed to get an empirical tradition established. The nature of his social statistical studies themselves in part are an answer to this question. First, they were mostly based on the crime and suicide statistics of Tönnies' own home province of Schleswig-Holstein and had thus somewhat of a local flavor.[10] Second, his presentation and notation were extremely involved, and amidst the maze of numbers, correlations and computations the larger purpose of the studies could easily become lost. Third, Tönnies tackled problems of data analysis which would have required for their satisfactory solution a working knowledge of statistical techniques such as the correlation between time series, multiple regression, and factor analysis, which at the time even the mathematically oriented statisticians were just getting familiar with, and which his techniques and methodology, despite his ingenuity and inventiveness, did not measure up to. Lastly, he did not bring his own rich theoretical notions to bear systematically upon his computational work. His statistical monographs are impressive for their computational virtuosity, but do not constitute an interlocking of theory with qualitative observation and quantitative results.

Tönnies' enthusiasm for exact social statistical investigations was of long standing.[11] In his recently published correspondence with

[10] The choice of concentrating on a delimited geographical area was not dictated by convenience alone. Tönnies thought that one of the serious defects of Mayr's social statistics were the broad, crossnational comparisons the latter was so fond of presenting, because the wide discrepancies in the collection and classification of the data made the figures too imprecise and misleading for comparative purposes.
[11] Tönnies was interested in criminology, juvenile delinquency, and crime statistics already in his student days. He was a frequent reviewer of the literature on crimi-

the philosopher and educator Friedrich Paulsen there are references to his plans for quantitative investigations as far back as 1880 [74, p. 70; pp. 86-7]. He was also outspoken in his admiration for Quetelet (p. 233). But already in 1903 Tönnies foresaw that his accomplishments would not measure up to his earlier expectations and the effort he was spending on these investigations (p. 373): '...as to my work in moral statistics I am afraid that the mouse which will jump out in the end will disappoint you and others, as is sometimes the case with results that were a long time in the making... I often think that I might have spent all this precious time more fruitfully.' It remains somewhat of a mystery why Tönnies was not able to, or did not want to, enlist the collaboration of a mathematical statistician which might have produced results as fruitful as the collaboration of Galton and Pearson.

Tönnies' empirical work was actually not confined to these monographs. At the turn of the century he wrote an extensive account of the great strike in the port of Hamburg in 1896-97 [138] which was based on secondary sources as well as his own eyewitness experiences of the events he reported. His description of the power structure in the port, with a group of small independent operators blurring the sharp contrast between the entrepreneurs and the workers, was definitely sociological and not merely journalistic. He attributed for example the lack of an organized labor movement before the strike (p. 228) 'in part to the circumstances that the possibility of transition from worker to capitalist has been preserved here more than in other branches of work, which again is connected with the presence of the mediating independent operators.' He explained the solidarity of longshoremen and sailors by the ties between them. The youth in the port-area were still attracted to the high seas, and when they had become thoroughly disillusioned they could fall back upon dock work as a natural secondary line of retreat.

Tönnies also participated in the 1902 Verein für Sozialpolitik survey on the condition of workers and sailors on seafaring ships [139]. He wrote a detailed 6-page report which outlined to the other Verein researchers the items that were to be clarified. Most of the twelve sections of his outline covered the usual topics of wages, living conditions, work hours, legal rights, illness, etc., but section K on 'moral conditions' dwelt concretely with social relations on board ship [152,

---

nology in the 1890s [136]. But his first social-statistical monograph [141] was not published until 1909.

CIII, p. x]: 'Is there some sort of solidarity which binds the officer and the crew together? What is the tenor of interpersonal relations (between the two groups)? at the expense of the fire-men?...' Tönnies himself surveyed the seamen of Kiel and Lübeck. Both of these early studies are however peripheral to the mainstream of his empirical efforts.

Tönnies acquired his statistical skills from Ernst Engel, who also probably introduced him to the ideas and works of Adolph Quetelet.[12] Tönnies did not, however, accept Quetelet's ideas uncritically. In an 1895 paper entitled 'Crime as a social phenomenon' [137], he was critical of the notion of 'disposition to crime.' It is not possible to demonstrate from criminal statistics the decline of this disposition with increasing age because (p. 337) incarceration tends to shorten the life of convicted criminals, thus producing a decline in age-specific crime rates. Moreover the criminal 'career' is such that as the criminal grows older, he tends to retreat into marginal criminal occupations that are not *per se* illegal, but still aid the younger criminals to pursue their profession sucessfully. Finally nothing is known about the emigration of the professional criminal population. Repeated criminal acts by the same person also are misleading in this respect (pp. 335-336) for it is impossible to distinguish the professional criminal from those repeaters who by virtue of their occupation are exposed over and over again to the same opportunity and temptation, like domestic servants. Tönnies introduced the distinction between 'crimes of opportunity' and 'crimes of habit'. Crimes of habit occur in all strata of the population and have remained constant over centuries, whereas (p. 341) 'the great mass of small and planless crimes have steadily increased with the dissolution of 'Volk-Gemeinschaft' and the proletarization of the masses.' Thus Tönnies distinguished between a basic and constant minimum of crime in society which was of a pathological nature, partly due to hereditary and partly due to social factors, and the great bulk of socially generated criminal acts that could be traced to 'great inequalities in economic and moral condition' between the proletarian and the other strata, such as unemployment, alcoholism, migratory life, etc. Tönnies' formulation combined to some extent his own ideas on social change with Quetelet's notion

---

[12] Tönnies once referred to Engel as the man [150, p. 547] 'whom I like to remember as my teacher...,' and to Quetelet [151, p. 439] 'as that excellent Belgian, astronomer by profession, who became one of the founders of sociography....'

of a criminal disposition. He did not make clear, however, whether professional criminals were the result of hereditary factors or of the transition from rural community to urban society. His own moral statistical monographs were an attempt to show quantitatively which combination of social factors were favoring or impeding the production of various types of crime.

In 1909 Tönnies published the method of association he had used since 1896 and illustrated it on criminal statistics from Schleswig-Holstein [141]. The purpose of the investigation was to determine the geographical origin of criminals and to correlate the incidence of criminality with other characteristics of the counties in which they were born. For each of the counties, further separated into an urban and a rural part, he established three criminal rates: PD, the incidence of thieves; PS, the incidence of sexual offenders; and PV, the incidence of other criminals. Tönnies then established meticulously county rates for some 39 other variables. These included 'moral characteristics' such as the percent of illiterates, the infant mortality for illegitimate children, suicide rate, the average number of inhabitants per dwelling, etc. The 'agrarian characteristics' of the counties were described in six variables according to the percent of total cultivated acreage consolidated into holdings of 100 or more hectares, 50–100 ha, 10–50 ha, 2–10 ha, 1–2 ha, or 0–1 ha. Tönnies kept the notions of 'concept' and 'indicator' distinct in his mind, but apparently held that each concept had but *one* indicator. For example among his variables he distinguished between 'income tax,' 'a positive characteristic for relative wealth,' and 'class-taxes,' 'a positive indicator for relative well-being,' whereas today a sociologist would probably regard both of these indicators as being drawn from a much larger pool of possible indicators of the same concept that might be termed the wealth or material well being of a county. Tönnies did not *a priori* limit himself to variables that could be expressed quantitatively (p. 705): 'To a truly scientific social statistics should belong the task of characterizing sharply each district, each city of a county by its enduring features, preferably in a statistical way, but also through other descriptive features.' Despite the fact that his method of association did not require quantitative variables, all the features which Tönnies singled out to characterize his collectivities with (the counties of Schleswig-Holstein) were of the analytic type, that is expressible in numerical rates. Had Tönnies carried out his own ideas he would not have split the agrarian characteristics into the six variables mentioned above (which are not independent anyway, since a high proportion of large farms excludes the possibility of a high proportion of medium-sized holdings), instead of describing the modal pattern of agricultural enterprise in the counties as a single variable. Such a procedure would have simplified his analysis considerably since he would have had to contend with one rather than six interdependent relationships between agricultural features and crime rates.

With respect to the data Tönnies had assembled, he noticed that (p. 709) 'on the surface, the criminal rates are higher for the cities than for the countryside... there are many such differences which the statisticians customarily are content to observe. The task as I see it is to establish more exact relationships... to give them a numerical expression.' His measure of association – called 'correlation' by Tönnies since he thought it was a simpler version, but similar to the Pearson correlation coefficient – was actually based on rank order, and was not grounded on any probabilistic foundation.[13] Tönnies computed more than 100 association measures from his data, each of his independent variables with PD, PV and PS, in both urban and rural areas. He noticed that for each independent variable the sign of the six associations was usually the same, whereupon he computed an average score for each and briefly discussed them in turn, promising the reader that he would pursue the analysis further in a later publication.

In 1924 Tönnies pushed his analysis of the Schleswig-Holstein criminal figures somewhat further [144]. Most of the variables and notation were still the same, the procedure, however, differed somewhat. He now ranked always 4 sets of 10 counties along some variable

---

[13]   Tönnies would rank order the 20 counties of Schleswig-Holstein by two variables, for example population density and PD, the incidence of thieves. For each variable he would split the 20 ranked counties into 5 categories, A, B, C, D and E, each containig 4 counties with the 4 highest in category A, etc., and then would classify each county into the 5 by 5 table measure thus constructed with the marginals of the table along both variables held artificially equal to 4. The procedure and the measure of association were geared to the 20 counties of Schleswig-Holstein, and Tönnies never generalized it to another than 20. The measure of association itself would consist of adding the entries along the main diagonal, weighted by a factor of 2, to the entries in its two off-diagonals and then subtracting the entries of the minor diagonal, again weighted by 2, and the entries in its off-diagonals. The measure might vary between +32 and —32, perfect positive to negative association, and was easily computed by mere addition and substraction.

(separating the Schleswig and Holstein counties, and then the rural and urban parts of each county). Instead of the 5 categories A to E he worked with the dichotomies High and Low, but this again was a simplified ranking rather than a dichotomized metric scale as the first five of the ten ranked counties were always High on the variable. The measure of association now used was a simple percent-difference in a 2 x 2 table, that is the H-H entry minus the H-L entry expressed as a percent difference.[14] Again more than 100 such percent differences were computed, the average of each variable taken over the four sets of counties, and these averages finally ranked by the degree of their association with PD, the incidence of thieves. At this point Tönnies pushed the analysis further to check what the combined effect of two variables might be upon PD (in his shorthand notation represented by symbols such as ES+KS:PD), and developed a numerical measure for it which was the percent difference of the entries in H-H-H and H-H-L.[15] Then he ranked many such combinations of two variables according to the degree of their combined effect upon PD; in fact he tried to expand his method to include the effect of more than two variables combined. The final conclusion from this multitude of figures was that the combinations of 'well-being' and 'low occupancy per dwelling,' W+H, as well as 'well-being' and 'low illegitimacy rate', W+M were in all four sets of counties negatively associated with the productivity of thieves. It is a good example of the kind of empirical law that Tönnies was able to extract from the data, and the fact that he did not point out its connection with a body of theory.

In subsequent monographs on crime in Schleswig-Holstein published in 1927 [145] and 1929 [146], Tönnies pursued his earlier line of analysis, but he also made some changes that brought his computations closer to his theoretical notions. Instead of the three-way classification of criminals, PD, PS, and PV, he used the dichotomy 'rogues' and 'offenders'. The 'rogues' included thieves, swindlers, and robbers, or those criminals who act with a calculated purpose. The 'offenders' included arsonists, perjurors, sexual offenders, and vandals, or those criminals who act from a brutal, immediate, egotistic drive. Tönnies was able to demonstrate on the basis of his tables and calculations

---

[14] This is correct since the percent difference H–H minus H–L is a complete characterization of a 2 × 2 table in the case of fixed marginals.

[15] This is incorrect since the entries in L–L–H and L–L–L also have to be included in a measure of the combined effect of two stratifiers upon a third variable.

that [145, pp. 804-805] 'the probability that a criminal was born in an urban area is the greater – in Schleswig-Holstein – the nearer the criminal act is to 'roguishness,' namely that it originates in a conscious and sustained will, and that it is not an occasional but a usual means of making a living. The probability of urban origin is smaller in proportion as the criminal act is more likely to stem from an irrational passion, even if it is based on self-interest or a wild desire. In just the opposite way the probability of rural origin increases or decreases'.

Tönnies' most complete monograph on suicide was published in 1927 with the subtitle 'a statistical-sociological study' [149]. It was divided into two parts. In the first part (pp. 7-30) he established and analyzed trends in age- and sex-specific suicide rates, in the counties and districts of Schleswig-Holstein from the early 19th century up to the post-war period. His method was essentially impressionistic and his explanations of a common-sense nature. Noting the increase in male suicide rates in 1919-20 he wrote for example (p. 29): 'Even in the rural areas the increase is marked. One is tempted to relate this fact to the well-known events of these years, namely the inflation and the losses of wealth, but these suppositions are necessarily vague; only a questioning of local authorities and the clergy might shed light on the matter.' The second part of the monograph (pp. 31-63) was similar in method and intent to the studies on crime described earlier. For each of the 20 counties of Schleswig-Holstein, Tönnies established urban and rural, male and female, average suicide rates on the basis of figures from the years 1876-1910. Next he characterizes the counties along 44 different variables – agriculture, demographic, moral statistical, economic – the same ones he had used earlier. Then using his method of rank order association he computed 264 measures of association, each of the 44 independent variables with the 6 dependent suicide rates, and included them in a table (pp. 46-47). Finally he analyzed the relationships in the table (pp. 47-60) without successfully getting around the fundamental problem of the intercorrelation of the 44 county characteristics. His conclusions (pp. 60-64) were again commonsense explanations. Noting the intercorrelation of suicide, illegitimacy, illiteracy, and crowded tenements, he called suicide a social-pathological phenomenon of proletarian life-conditions.

Unlike Durkheim whose study of suicide was intimately related to his theoretical concern with moral integration and the binding power of norms upon individuals in various groups and social contexts,

Tönnies did not relate his moral statistical material to his own theoretical notions systematically. He was confined by the nature of his data to starting with the number of criminals or suicides in each county of Schleswig-Holstein for each year. Tönnies converted the absolute numbers into average rates; moreover his procedure of picking a large number of county features and characterizing each feature numerically to study its relationship to crime and suicide was fundamentally sound. At this point rather than introducing his rank order association method of studying each county variable for its association with the dependent variable separately, he might have attempted to construct a typology or continuum of Gemeinschaft and Geselleschaft for the counties, and thus introduced certain theoretically relevant notions.[16]

Tönnies was, however, aware of his own shortcomings and that of any single individual, for that matter, attempting to tackle such problems alone. All of his later monographs, [149], [150], [151]- end with a plea for the creation of 'moral statistical' or 'sociographic observatories' financed by the government, where the 'facts of social life, especially those of moral significance, might be studied scientifically.' These observatories would have to be independent of any administrative apparatus (unlike the statistical bureaus) so that they might pursue pure scientific research free of outside demands and pressures. Tönnies envisaged cooperation among many professionals and specialists, sociologists, statisticians, doctors, ministers, schoolteachers, and even educated women of the privileged strata, who after a period of training in sociographic and statistical methods, would make a concerted research effort in the area of all social-pathological phenomena such as crime, suicide, prostitution, alcoholism, juvenile delinquency, etc., using all manner of empirical methods, from precise measurement to observation and estimation. Tönnies was unsuccessful

[16] This typology might have been constructed in two different ways: characterizing the basic concepts themselves in terms of the county features for which data was available, performing reduction operations and then classifying the counties by degree of 'Gemeinschaft' or according to types; alternatively a typology might have been generated by means of a mathematical procedure (as in factor analysis) applied to the matrix of correlations between the features. Both of these procedures were, of course, in their early beginnings at the time and used only by a small number of social scientists. It is also doubtful that the variables and numerical indicators which Tönnies had avaiblable would have done full justice to the rich notions of 'Gemeinschaft' and 'Gesellschaft.' But a typology or continuum 'urban-rural' probably might have been constructed.

in these efforts. Only single individuals continued the type of social statistical investigation that he pursued all his life.[17] At the 1930 meetings of the German Sociological Society of which Tönnies had been elected life-long president, there was for the first time a section on sociography, yet no empirical paper was presented at it.

It should be mentioned finally that besides monographs on crime and suicide, Tönnies investigated a wide range of other topics as well by means of his statistical methods.[18] In 1910 he published a study of agricultural statistics on land tenure and size of farms in the 20 counties of Schleswig-Holstein [142]. Here he listed twenty agricultural characteristics, rather than the earlier six. Most of the study was an attempt to find some patterns in the 20 x 19 associations of each variable with all of the others, yet Tönnies did not in the end reduce them into a typology. In 1915 he published an investigation of the fluctuations in German marriage rates from 1841 to 1912 [143], thought he had detected a four-year periodic up and down movement in them, and proceeded to examine some economic time series such as the price of grains, the interest rate, the total income of the railroads, etc., in view of detecting a corresponding periodicity. This study of cyclical changes was one of the first German contributions to the empirical study of business cycles. His method of approaching the problem was essentially to convert the series of numbers or rates into a series of + and — signs, depending upon whether or not the rate had exceeded the level of the preceding year. Then he would look for some even intervals in which the signs tended to be the same, in his case intervals of four years, split the entire series of some 70 years into intervals of eight years, designated the first four years in each interval as H (for hohe, high) and the remaining four as N (for niedere, low). Finally he computed the proportion of + and — signs in each of the two sets of years H and N, and speculated on whether the prevalence of + or — signs could be due to chance alone. To be sure

[17] Rudolf Heberle published a number of social statistical monographs in the 1920s and 1930s on migration and population movements in Germany and the U.S., some of which were supported by the Rockefeller Foundation. Heberle also wrote the entry 'sociography' in the 1931 Handbook of Sociology edited by Vierkandt.

[18] Jacoby [71, p. 145] reports that Tönnies' unpublished social statistical papers are available in the archives of the Institute for World Economics at the University of Kiel. An examination of this unpublished material might perhaps answer some of the questions on Tönnies' empirical work that were raised in this chapter.

in the absence of tests of significance the mode of analysis was impressionistic, yet there was a definite system in the way Tönnies went about it and even today the statistical methods of establishing periodicities or correlations between time series is by no means solved satisfactorily. The mere fact of looking at fluctuations in the marriage rate, rather than establishing its constancy over the years, was a departure from the earlier procedure of the moral statisticians.

In 1924 Tönnies published an article entitled 'The correlation between parties in the statistics of the Reichstag elections of the city of Kiel' [147], an application of his method to voting. He was interested in finding relationships between the ways the seven major parties had fared in various sections of the city. To that end he divided the city into five groups of 25 electoral precincts, for each party he ranked the precincts by the size of the vote, then computed his measure of association between each pair of parties. He concluded that 'all bourgeois parties are positively related to each other' – that is, regardless of their total strenght they would do relatively well or poorly in the same districts – whereas the greatest negative association was between the largest bourgeois party, the Deutschnationalepartei, and the largest proletarian party, the Social Democrats.

Tönnies was not the only social scientist interested in a closer collaboration between sociology and statistics. At the first meeting of the German Sociological Society in 1910, a section on statistics was formed at the initiative of professional statisticians interested in a closer collaboration between the two disciplines. One of them, the Austrian statistician Franz Zizek, wrote a short book *Statistics and Sociology* [180] which summarized matters as they stood just before the World War and throws light on the consequences of the intellectual division of labor that had occurred since the time of Quetelet. Zizek deplored the relative lack of quantitative data in the works of the German sociologists, by whom he meant men like Schaeffle, Eisler, Gumplowitz and others, and correctly noted that Tönnies alone was an exception. At the same time he pointed to a gap between the two fields which in retrospect is not as wide as it seemed to him (p. 6): 'By the very nature of the statistical method, statistics can only grasp countable and measurable facts; its object is the establishment of what is dimensional in society.... Sociology on the other hand is interested in many other things which can never be grasped directly in a statistical manner: systems of law, customs and mores, religions and myths, relationships of power, political movements and many similar things.' Zizek saw for example that much useful data on social stratification was being turned out by the statistical bureaus, namely income distributions and occupation statistics, but warned that (p. 25) 'statistics must naturally limit itself to statistically graspable characteristics, whereas for sociology other characteristics like social prestige might come into consideration... for example individuals in a lower income group may still enjoy higher social status in some ways than those at higher income level.' This distinction between economic and social ranking was a good sociological insight into the problem of social class, but citing 'social prestige' as an example of a variable which cannot be quantified was an unfortunate advice. Subsequent developments have shown that variables that can be rank ordered are also amenable to scaling techniques. Nor is it true that statistics is confined to dealing with quantities and quantifiable variables such as age and income. Yule had already at the time introduced the notion of attribute statistics. But Zizek could not advise social scientists to use sampling methods because these developments were largely unknown even to the statisticians themselves.

Another statistician Ferdinand Schmid in a 1916 article [118] reviewing the history of social research in Europe during the past century also came to the conclusion that greater collaboration between statisticians and social scientists would be both desirable and fruitful. He, like Tönnies, realized that the work to be done transcended the abilities and energies of single individuals, and called for the creation of an Institute for the Study of Society. Still another statistician Schöne [120] two years later noted the importance of establishing an empirical-sociological science as a foundation for all the disciplines dealing with social relations and institutions. He noted the widening gap in the course of the 19th century between the administrative statistics of the government statistical bureaus and scientific research at the universities, and advocated the enlargement of the social science seminars to statistical-sociological institutes, giving students an opportunity to acquire experience in the statistical bureaus and their professors a chance to use wider facilities for scientific surveys.

IV. *Field methods and the university seminars*

The technique of direct observation is not at all particular to modern social research. Since the time of the great voyages of exploration a steady stream of books on non-western cultures written mostly by travelers and missionaries had been avidly read in all Europe. During the Enlightenment it became even fashionable to disguise indictments of the *ancien régime* or of civilization itself in a literary form inspired by these accounts, as Montesquieu's *Lettres Persanes* or Diderot's Bougainville dialogue will testify. The remarkable development of anthropology in 19th century England can be understood in the light of the availability of first hand reports form her colonies and of the administrative encouragement to engage in field work. Germany was, on the other hand, without colonies till the end of the century. The incentive for field work originated in the romantics' discovery of the notion of *Volk*, which brought with it a positive evaluation of the beliefs and customs of the German peasantry. The peasants were thought to embody the genuine traditions and national character of the German people in its uncorrupted form. Since the time of the Grimm brothers a number of researchers were criss-crossing the land, noting down dialects and fairy tales as well as observing dress, customs and inscriptions in the village houses and churches. Often the main interest behind these activites was to trace the genealogy of superstitions and tales back to the myths and sagas of pagan times, and not to obtain an unbiased account of contemporary village life. A man like Mannhardt in the sixties was conscious of a race against time in collecting this material for genuine rural life was disappearing all around him. He even thought of organizing a great census of Volk-traditions by sending circulars to every village school-teacher in Germany [94]. For example question # 22 read: 'Do you have in your district tales about flying dragons, dwarfs, cobolds, witches, who steal the grain from the peasant's field to take it to others through the air?' Mannhardt was apparently successful in collecting several thousand replies.

Growing out of the romantic tradition but directed more to immediate social and political problems was the work of Wilhelm Heinrich
von Riehl. He had studied theology, cultural and art history, and was
influenced by the political theories of Justus Möser. From 1846 to
1854 he pursued a successful journalistic career, and starting in 1853
published a four-volume work based on his travels entitled *The Natural
History of the Volk as the Foundation of German Social Policy* [112]. Three
years later the fourth edition was already in print, and many more were
to follow. Riehl was a political conservative who advocated a revival
of the estate system which the 1848 revolution almost succeeded in
toppling, championed the idea of administrative decentralization and
above all the revival of the old patriarchal family in which the key
virtues were authority, piety and simplicity. He detested the French
encyclopedists and the 'age of the wig' during which simple German
customs became corrupted. His success no doubt was that he captured
the post-revolutionary mood and gave it a clear expression.

Riehl is, however, mentioned here not because of his political views
or his popularity, but his notion of *Volkskunde* as an empirical science.
The purpose of the study of the Volk was to discover the laws of Volk-
life which were to serve as an empirical foundation for political science
and the policies of the statesman. The way to discover these laws was
through direct observation of the people [113, p. 17]: 'Especially the
research directed at contemporary Volk-life is inadequate when
performed on secondary sources. Whoever wants to represent the
individuality of the Volk only through the data that are in libraries,
archives or statistical bureaus will put together but a rattling skeleton
and not a picture that breathes life. For that purpose first hand
sources are necessary, and they can only be gotten by walking through
the country on one's own feet.' Elsewhere Riehl was equally explicit
in his critique of the dominant tradition of documenting contemporary
social life [112, III, p. 87]: 'Our statisticians calculate dutifully...
the average number of heads per family, the number of marriages
each year, and how many single people live outside of family life.
This is a useful body of knowledge, yet should this remain our entire
knowledge of the sexes and the family? The statesman should not
only be permitted to look into the church registers, but be allowed
into the house itself.'

Riehl himself spent years of travel to every corner of the country,
but despite his outspoken advocacy for empirical method and his

descriptive travel reports he did not provide the reader with a well thought out and scientifically detached analysis of a total society in the Tocqueville manner. His work was rather a moralistic indictment of society filled with proverbial wisdom and generalizations. The explanatory principle in Riehl often boiled down to 'tendencies' inherent in the Volk-character, without regard to the social structure and the institutions of the community. Nonetheless Riehl was one of the first social scientists to be quite explicit about his method of observation and research. The introductory chapter of the final volume in his series, a collection of some of his travel essays with the title *The Book of Travel* [112, IV], was devoted to the description of his field methods, or 'the trade secrets of the study of the Volk' as he called it.

To justify his empirical method Riehl wrote (p. 21): 'It is said today that in our time statistical studies can only be made in administrative offices, that one needs no longer travel to gather statistics, and that a traveling statistician has become an absurdity.... Even if one no longer has to travel to collect numbers, a statistician should still travel in order to get an understanding for the numbers, in order to discover the threads of interrelationships in the numerical data used to describe Volk-life which are not written down in the official documents.' His own method was simply contained in a few rules. Extensive preparations should precede a statistical trip (p. 7) so that one knew more about the history and present condition of the region than even the majority of the educated inhabitants,[1] and that one would not become lost nor need ask anyone for the right way. Travel should be on foot (p. 3) and alone (p. 5). Riehl's only companions were his dog, a map, and his diary into which (pp. 19-20) 'I do not want to write subjective impressions and experiences, but an objective account of the region's character clarified and brought to life by walking and listening on location,' unlike the diaries of the 18th century 'when a description of land and people was used primarily as a pretext to present one's own self to the reader.' Each region has a 'signature,' a characteristic global feature (p. 16), 'that must become the knot to which the entire tissue of our research and description is to be fastened.' Riehl was especially aware of the problems of obtaining useful information from people by direct questioning. While

---

[1] 'Four weeks of preparation for two weeks of foot travel is not unreasonable.'

it was relatively simple to question educated people, provided one was familiar with the region, to handle the illiterates was a more delicate matter (p. 11): 'What the peasant tells us is only a matter of good luck and circumstances; it has sometimes much value, more often little or no value whatsoever. Yet the way in which the peasant talks about himself, what his feelings are, and how he exercises judgment, often reveal us the sharpest and most basic features in the character of the Volk. Instead of questioning the peasant I prefer to tell him about the far away world and thus get him to volunteer statements.... I lead him to matters that I am interested to hear and not those he prefers to talk about. To tell people stories opens their own heart in turn; whoever questions them as in an examination will make them shut their mouth.' Riehl also made a practice to honor the anonymity of his informants (p. 25). What distinguished Riehl's method from present day participant observation and field methods was that he did not remain in any one place for an intensive study, but like a traveler was always passing through the area without sharing the inhabitants' way of life.

The most important volume in the quartet was the third one entitled *The Family* [112, III]. It was almost entirely devoted to document the 'dissolution of family consciousness.' Signs of it were evident everywhere (p. 145): 'The name no longer characterizes the personality, the family, the estate, or the occupation. It becomes purely an outward enumeration, and when an honest tailor christens his children Athelstan, Jean-Noe and Oscar, or Natalie, Zaïre, Olga and Iphigenie, then it is just like giving them numbers for these names are just as lifeless as dead numbers.' Another indication was the frequent practice of inviting guests out to a restaurant rather than serving them dinner in one's own house. Should the guest however come to the house, one makes every effort to hide the 'ways of the house' (p. 161): 'Of a hundred families in which a prayer is still being said at table, ninety-nine will not say it when a guest is present... the children are dismissed, the maids have to rearrange the room beforehand, the cat and the dog have to leave the fireplace, the entire house becomes topsy-turvy.' Houses no longer are known by their name or the inscription over the front door, but by their streetnumber (p. 184); the 'salon' has become the most carefully kept room in the house in order to keep up the pretence of being a member of good society (pp. 174-175); instead of a family chronicle each member keeps his

own private diary (p. 264). An encouraging sign of the 'revival of
the family spirit' is, however, the custom of the open house evening
when once a week the entire family is at home to receive whatever
acquaintances chance to drop in (p. 246).

Upon reading Riehl today, one has the feeling that he paid too
much attention to the more outward manifestations of social change
such as the changing manners and fashions, and not enough to the
capitalist and industrial transformation taking place all around him.
In Germany as elsewhere this transformation was receiving a powerful
human impetus through the entrepreneur who wished to hand down
the family firm to his sons. Thomas Mann's *Buddenbrooks* provides
greater insight into the driving spirit behind the bourgeois family of
19th century Germany than Riehl. Still the notion of studying
contemporary society by direct observation in the field remains an
important and original contribution.

After 1854 Riehl himself settled down into an academic career at
Munich and his work became more and more concerned with the
description of rural life exclusively. In the 1860s he was editor of a
five-volume documentary of Bavaria which was a mixture of geology
geography, linguistics, customs, beliefs and myths, art history, and
demographic statistics. What in later years became known as *Landes
und Volksforschung* was increasingly a combination of geography, botany,
meteorology, and physical anthropology than social research. At
most one was advised to observe the ratio of blondes to brunettes in
a village to determine racial composition, and make drawings of
typical peasant houses to trace ancient Germanic and Celtic influences.
Another offshoot was the end of the century literature on scientific
and colonial expeditions whose manuals usually contained a slim
chapter on 'anthropological observation,' meaning a list of 200 or so
body measurements to be perfomed on the first native who might
submit to such torture.

Independent of Riehl and the *Volkskunde* tradition inspired by the
romantic movement there developed in Germany somewhat later a
literature on the condition of the peasantry and the working classes
which was pursued primarily from the universities by certain economists and their seminar students. By the latter part of the 19th century
the German universities all had a political economy department which
had splintered from earlier departments where public administration
was taught for prospective civil servants. The backbone of the curricu-

lum was political economy and public finance; slowly topics like 'socialism' and 'the working class question' became included in the curriculum. By the late eighties most departments offered a political economy seminar where the students could write a thesis on contemporary issues besides the more traditional social and economic history [90, pp. 219 ff.]. Men like Schmoller and Brentano were responsible in getting these seminars started. Brentano ran a seminar in Strassburg with Knapp, then founded one in Leipzig in 1889 and in Munich in 1891 where he finally settled down for over 25 years. Schmoller founded the Berlin seminar upon his appointment to the faculty there in 1882. The seminars were endowed with sums from a few hundred marks to nearly 2,000 M for Berlin and Munich [90, p. 400], which was just enough to purchase books and subsidize the publication of the better theses in such series as the *Münchner Volkswirtschaftliche Abhandlungen*, edited by Brentano and the *Staats und Sozialwissenschaftliche Forschungen*, edited by Schmoller. The topic of those studies which were of a sociological nature was invariably some aspect of the condition of the rural and urban lower class in a city or rural district. In both method and substance these theses were rather unimaginative and stereotyped products. They did in part make use of field observation as a means of securing or checking data, although no student ever spent more than a few weeks during school holidays in the region he was reporting on.[2] The main core was invariably the usual statistics on wages, food prices, slum dwellings, mortality, and the inevitable section on moral conditions containing the figures on illegitimacy and crime.

---

[2] In the post-war years Leopold von Wiese continued the tradition of taking field trips with students of his seminar during the holidays, from which several publications on rural social structure resulted. Wiese was, however, under no illusion about the inherent limitations of this form of organized social research. In a 1934 book review [172] of the *Unemployed of Marienthal*, a study undertaken by a Viennese group of social psychologists under the direction of Lazarsfeld, he wrote; 'I am aware of how similar my own attempts are with the efforts of the Viennese sociographers. I would, if I had enough time and money at my disposal, proceed in the same way on the main as they have.... My own attempts must remain for the time being of a purely pedagogic-didactic sort; they can only hope that in the short nine or ten days around Pentecost the students living in small groups with the village inhabitants will receive a certain amount of stimulation and guidance which will be useful to them in later investigations. For the Viennese researches, theoretically schooled and scientifically advanced observers were able to devote a long period of time entirely to the task of achieving valuable scientific results which went beyond the limits of training students.'

To illustrate the kinds of observations made at this time one might mention a study published in 1879 by Alphons Thun [135] on the industries and the workers in the lower Rhein region which was for many years considered a model of the regional survey for Schmoller's students writing their theses or first book. Thun wrote in the introduction that 'in Aachen my stay extended from March to June 1878; I have criss-crossed the city on all its streets, visited pubs and entertainment places and over a hundred workers' apartments, always in company of civil servants and policemen, doctors, ministers or workers....' The study contained very little actual first hand observation. In an exceptional passage Thun described a visit to a local pub in which he was accompanied by a policeman in these words (p. 55): 'The public is rather well behaved and entertains itself in a subdued tone. But the penetrating look of the police officer gets inside the inner core of each person: the ex-convict shudders and asserts that he has found employment here; a few well known thieves bury their noses into their glasses; the prostitutes jump up and quickly leave; the bums look around suspiciously; only the honest beggars and unemployed workers look up openly to us....' All this reads very much like a second rate mystery story, yet Thun was completely earnest in writing these lines. The whole idea of going into a disreputable pub to make observations on the 'moral condition' of the lower class in company of a police officer sounds very naive today. Thun must have been unfamiliar and puzzled by his subject matter. When the owner of the pub explained to him that the nicer back room of the pub was reserved for those who could afford to pay for their dinner, whereas all those who could not afford a meal were kept crowded in the front room so as not to disturb the paying customers, he wrote in genuine amazement: 'Amidst all this misery there are still class differences!'

A work of a different sort was that of Gottlieb Schnapper-Arndt,[3] who actually lived in the field with his subjects when he was studying them. Schnapper-Arndt was, however, an exception in many ways. He was related to the Frankfurt branch of the Rothschild family and did not have to work for a living [24, p. 209]. As a young man in Ernst Engels' statistical seminar, he was exposed to the ideas of Le

---

[3] Schnapper-Arndt's participation in the Verein für Sozialpolitik surveys and his methodological critique of the usury survey have already been discussed above (see Chap. II, sec. 2.).

Play on family monographs and budgets to which he subsequently devoted all his life as an unaffiliated, private researcher. One might even go so far as to say that he developed an obsession for exact budget measurements. His most complete field study was a monograph on five rural communities in the Taunus hills [122] subtitled ' a social statistical investigation of small peasantry, cottage industry and Volk-life.' He had visited these villages already in the mid-seventies, then spent the entire spring and fall of 1881 living there to complete his observations. 'Reports on the condition of the people in the cottage industries, especially by K. Marx, awakened in me the desire to see the truth for myself,' he wrote in the introduction. On the theoretical side, he conceived of the study as 'a miniature-statistical description of my villages,' the significance of which he hoped would be that 'the exact investigation of a delimited object in some cases will reveal the influence of social factors at least as surely as mass observations.' Schnapper-Arndt collected his own miniature data wherever the information was unavailable. For example a table (p. 95) entitled 'overview of the industrial activity of schoolchildren in the mountain villages' classified all schoolchildren by age, type of work, and the starting and finishing hour of their work day, and was based on his own personal census. The poverty and backwardness of the villages is difficult to imagine but for the fact that it is so precisely documented. From a table on the living conditions for which he again surveyed every building (p. 118), it appears that more than 50 percent of the population lived in a room with five or more other people in it. From a detailed table based on the military draft records of five years (pp. 154-155), it appears that 62.3 percent of all males were unfit for military service because of 'general body weakness, hernia, varicose veins... and other deformities.' Schnapper-Arndt was especially complete on demography. There were mortality tables, diagrams of the age composition of the population, tables showing age of husband and wife and the number of subsequent children. On the other hand the rather brief section on moral conditions again illustrates the absence of a social anthropological tradition in Germany. There was no account of the role of the minister and the schoolteacher in the community, no account of any form of community organization, associations and friendship circles, nor of emigration and the migration to the cities which must have been fairly important elements of social disorganization. Schnapper-Arndt did, however, go beyond the customary figures on the number of illegitimate births, etc., as he described the fate of newly-wed couples (pp. 166-167). Since the children of the poorer peasants worked for their parents without pay, they were unable to accumulate savings to start an independent household. Often they had to lead separate lives, each at the parents' home; occasionally they might be able to move into a room previously rented to an outsider by one of the families, but they would soon have to leave to make room for the next brother or sister who was getting married (and in those days of a dozen children per family, the age lag between children was around one year, unless some had died). The ignorance of the population was complete. Schnapper-Arndt went around asking people whether they had heard of Schiller and Frederic the Great and drew only blank stares or answers like 'he does not live here.' One exceptional schoolchild had heard of Charlemagne, but remembered him as the first Hapsburg emperor (p. 175).

The most elaborate part of the study was an appendix over a hundred pages long. It included among other things two family monographs with detailed budgets, an inventory of clothes of the entire family and of other possessions such as furniture, the itemized cost of a typical peasant house with a diagram of it obtained from a carpenter, the business budget of a nail-maker who worked in his family work-shop with his two sons. The influence of Le Play was explicitly acknowledged in the family monographs. The main categories of the budget followed Le Play's, but Schnapper-Arndt was more thorough and added a few refinements in the cost calculation. In the case of all such durables as clothing and furniture, the expected duration of their useful life was recorded and a certain depreciation cost of the article included in the budget. Thus the value of new clothes bought during the current year was not included in full for they would last beyond the year, whereas a fraction of the value of old clothes was shown as consumed since they had been used up in part. The items listed were so exhaustive that for the monograph of a propertyless road-worker's family they covered about ten pages. One item, for example, was 'raspberries, picked on weekdays by the above named family members and on Sunday by the youngest daughter, for home consumption; 14 liters, at six pennies a liter according to estimates in the village... 0.84 Marks.' Schnapper-Arndt spent thirty sessions of several hours in assembling the budget, 'and we measured, weighed, counted and inspected all that time... our discussions interested N. himself considerably "for one isn't really aware of how one lives".' The second budget, that of a typical 'middle class' family of that region, proved easier to assemble for it was able to use an account and expense booklet.[4]

Social research activities were also carried out in the seminars that Lujo Brentano conducted. Heinrich Herkner, later to become known for his work in labor economics [61] and his activities in the Verein für Socialpolitik, wrote a doctoral thesis in 1886 in the Strassburg seminar of Knapp and Brentano on the Alsatian cotton industries [60] for which he also carried out a private questionnaire survey to be answered directly by the workers themselves, for he distrusted the official statistics on child and woman labor derived entirely from information of the owners and managers. Herkner got into trouble with the police over it, and perhaps for that reason did not publish the questionnaire in the dissertation. Brentano himself occasionally took to field trips. In 1894 a controversy about the indebtedness of peasants and the loss of their land flared up and was blamed by some on the laws of inheritance and transfer of peasant land holdings. Brentano suspected that the peasant actually followed his own traditional practices in complete disregard of the law. He prevailed upon the Bavarian Ministry of Justice to conduct a survey on this matter among the rural public notaries. The returns were later analyzed by one of his seminar students [47]. In the meanwhile Brentano and his students took a walking journey through some rural districts to gain first hand knowledge of local conditions. When during the Vienna convention of the Verein für Sozialpolitik in 1894 the land inheritance question came up for debate, and he was accused of painting a materialistic picture of the

---

[4] Karl Bücher, to whom Schnapper-Arndt used to turn for advice during his early budget studies, wrote in 1906 after his death [26, p. 690]: 'Such expenditure of time could be made only by a man who disposed of this costly human commodity freely and without regard to material cares, and who in all naive innocence made demands on the precious time of others to the outer limits of possibility.' Besides numerous other family budgets and exhaustive studies of the lives of single individuals, Schnapper-Arndt also wrote on the methodology of surveys [123] and on his European travels [124] as well as on social and moral statistics [125], published posthumously. While his writings seemed to have been well known he exerted little actual influence on the development of social research. His contemporaries thought of him as a curiosity, some going so far as to attribute his preference and ability for painstaking, detailed, numerical investigation to biological characteristics inherited from the Rothschilds.

peasantry, Brentano drew upon the observations he had made during the trip in his defense. The city clothes worn by the peasants were 'a symptom of how the peasant is already becoming urbanized in his consumption patterns...' [152, LXI, pp. 279 ff.]. Those who still clung to the romantic image of the peasant in his traditional dress and bucolic way of life were out of touch with reality.

Brentano was, however, not the kind of man around whom a systematic empirical research tradition might develop. By temperament he was a fighting man, and involved up to his neck in controversial political issues. He was an excellent economic historian and expert on contemporary union movement. His lifelong acquaintance with working-class leaders gave him a first hand knowledge of matters concerning the working class. He underestimated the potentialities of the questionnaire survey as a scientific instrument and preferred the type of cross-examination of witnesses used by the British Royal Commissions for establishing the truth. In a 1914 publication in which he outlined his ideas on social research systematically [22], he listed the following pitfalls of questioning people: they will voice opinions, not facts; they will often have no first hand knowledge of the situation; they will have a faulty memory; they will generalize from single cases; they will distort according to preconceived notions; and they will falsify consciously if their own interests are threatened. He concluded therefore that (p. 77) 'if a survey is to be scientifically usable, it should be conducted as oral crossexamination. Written surveys are only appropriate in cases where the numerical frequency of certain already well-known activities is to be established, that is in statistical surveys.' There were always a few students in his Munich seminar who were doing studies on the condition of factory workers, but these were descriptive reports and no organized effort on the part of all the students was conducted. Moreover it was no easy task to have access to data from private firms and organizations in those days, and this was further complicated by Brentano's political sympathies for the labor unions. On this score Brentano complained [22, p. 80]: 'Unfortunately it has become customary today that the interested parties whom the economic researchers approach for data will ask in what sense they will make use of it, and if the researchers reply, with no predetermined intention but openly in order to establish the truth, then the data will not be supplied.'

One seminar study deserves to be singled out because it was a departure from the usual run of the mill description of worker and peasant conditions. It was written in 1919 for Weber's sociological seminar in Munich and was probably the first field study of political organizations. Wilhem Matte's *The Bavarian Peasant Councils* [95] was concerned with the extent and nature of peasant support for the Eisner government and his Workers' Councils during the brief post-war socialist tenure of power in Bavaria. Matte started working in the summer of 1919 when some peasant leaders were still in prison. His task was difficult for many documents had been destroyed during the fighting which unseated the Eisner government. He sent out several hundred questionnaires, some to members of the Workers' Councils about their relations with the peasant councils, and most of them to the peasant councils and associations themselves about their own activities and membership. He was able to show from the composition of these bodies that the richer peasants and mayors (and not the rural proletariat as one might expect) were over-represented with respect to their proportion in the total population.

V. *Empirical monographs in the years 1895-1914*

1. *Introduction*

During the period following the turn of the century, empirical work in the social sciences in Germany broadened both in scope and depth. The Verein für Sozialpolitik and the religious associations were joined by other organizations and groups in carrying out empirical surveys. Workers' associations conducted surveys with practical aims in mind. They felt the need to check and complement the figures of official statistical volumes in order to press for favorable legislation. Some of the most interesting advances, however, came from isolated innovators, the physicist Abbe, the librarian Hofmann, and above all the worker Levenstein. To understand the empirical studies of this period, it is necessary briefly to examine the problems they were intended to clarify. As in the period preceding 1895, most empirical work was still concerned with but one topic: the working classes. The two areas of major concern were the problem of work in the broadest sense, and the social psychology of the proletariat. But whereas earlier the religious organizations investigated the extent of religious faith of the worker, the secular researchers of the later period were more concerned with the general level of culture and education of the workers, and therefore were interested in his reading, his political ideas, his hopes and his awareness of his own situation in the world. Conversely the problem of work no longer meant exclusively the workers' standard of living, but took on a twofold aspect. On the one hand an economic and military aspect, on the other, a genuine humanitarian concern. The military and economic aspect was in part due to an increasing agitation for shorter working hours, and naturally the question whether or not this would reduce production and profits as some held, or on the contrary increase it, as others maintained, was hotly debated. The military and political ramifications of this question were whether Germany could successfully compete with the British given one or the other alternative and whether or not the hours and years spent in the factories would produce a generation of men unfit for military service. On the humanitarian side, the prospect of an ever increasing factory population, living in slums, bringing with it a dehumanized race of men, their fate tied to the machines they were tending and with no hope for a brighter future, loomed large in the minds of contemporaries.

Another powerful intellectual current which influenced the empirical studies of this period and inspired a whole series of elite and genealogical studies was social darwinism, eugenics, and social theories based on racial and biological principles. In Germany no great names such as those of Darwin, Spencer, Galton, Gobineau, and Huxley abroad ever became identified with these movements, but rather those of more specialized university professors, such as the zoologists Ernst Ziegler and Ernst Haeckel, the biologist Alfred Ploetz and the psychiatrist Wilhelm Schallmayer. Starting from the allegedly scientifically proven fact of the inheritance of both physical and intellectual characteristics, and drawing on the notions of natural selection and the struggle for survival, these men were fond of pointing out that the social legislation protecting the working classes from the selection process of nature was already producing a degeneration of the biologically fitter human type of the upper class and the educated [107]. Popularizers of racial theories such as Otto Ammon [5, pp. 21-22] went as far as attributing the downfall of the Roman Empire and the 1870-71 victory over France to the superiority of the youthful germanic races.

These ideas and their implications for social philosophy and policy stirred a great deal of interest which spread beyond the universities. On January 1, 1900, an anonymous grant of 30,000 Marks, an enormous sum at the time, was offered in a widely publicized competition for the ten best essays on the topic 'What do we learn from the principles of the theory of heredity for the political development and legislation of states?' [178, pp. 2-5]. In 1903 the jury composed of the zoologist Haeckel, the economist Conrad and the philosopher Fraas, were able to choose from 60 submitted essays, and it was indicative of the widespread interest that the eight essays finally honored with prizes were written by a minister, two doctors, an engineer, a playwright, an educator, an economist and a philosopher. The zoologist Ziegler subsequently published the prize winnig essays in a series entitled *Nature and Society*.

The attitude of the social scientists to the social darwinist movement was critical, yet they were often influenced by it. What they questioned was the generalization of a few findings from medical and psychological research on the inheritance of certain physical diseases and mental disorders to a firm dogma of the inheritance of most intellectual abilities and personality traits. What they resented most was the claim of the social darwinists that they had discovered the ultimate and basic principles for the explanation of society and social processes. In addition the crude ideological element in the statements of some social darwinists and biologists on the subject of social reform was also repelling to the generally reform minded social scientists who were fully aware of the political forces and economic pressure groups shaping the course of events. Tönnies [140] for example engaged in a lengthy polemic from 1905 to 1907 with the psychiatrist Schallmayer, the first prize winner of the contest. Both the interest and critical attitude of the social scientists was also evident at the first meeting of the German Sociological Society in 1910 when the biologist Ploetz, editor of the influential *Archiv für Rassen- und Gesellschaftsbiologie*, was asked to present his point of view as the principal speaker of the section devoted to 'race and society' [108]. During the debate which followed his address, all the leading sociologists took to the floor, and it is indicative that Ploetz's final speech was interrupted a dozen times by critical comments, mainly those of Max Weber. Weber's own attitude was summarized in a statement he made at that session (p. 156): 'What we (sociologists) expect from the racial-biologists and what we no doubt... will one day obtain from them, is the exact proof of concrete, single relationships, that is to say (the proof) of the overwhelming importance of concrete hereditary factors. That proof, gentlemen, is lacking up to now....'[1] Weber also deplored the almost 'utopian enthusasim' with which the proponents of these new theories were undertaking their studies and which was leading them to misunderstand the limits of the applicability of their investigations.

On the purely scientific side the studies of this period still suffer from the absence of any notion of statistical sampling in the selection of the objects of the investigation, although a general awareness of the existence of sampling problems led to the adoption of stratified design for some studies. At the same time the studies of these years are no

---

[1] Weber himself at this time in his study of industrial workers tried to find just such concrete, quantitative relationships between the productivity of workers and certain factors attributable to biological inheritance (see Chap. VI, sec. 3, below).

longer necessarily of the geographical, descriptive and fact-finding type, but one may observe the emergence of monographs on a limited topic treated in greater depth than before. Still it was with the analysis of the data that most researchers had considerable difficulty, and the art of condensing and synthesizing a mass of material into such a form that lends itself to easy and intelligent summary did not keep pace with other innovations. Here, however, we are sometimes faced with concrete empirical results that today might still be examined either for purely historical reasons or for drawing up comparisons with the present.

To illustrate the diversity of social research, a few broad trends will be sketched without entering into any details. There were first of all a number of descriptive statistical works on the condition of the working or lower classes in a given city, put together by civil servants employed by the statistical agencies of the German states and cities. These studies were based almost entirely on official statistical material reanalyzed more carefully and concentrated on a delimited geographical area. Publications such as that by Woerishoffer [175] and Hirschberg [66] are typical examples of this kind of work. There were invariably chapters based on extended crosstabulations of occupation, age, religion, illness, mortality, living quarters, education, wages, unemployment, workers' associations and family budgets.

Then the numerous associations for the welfare of the working classes occasionally embarked upon social surveys on limited problems. The Association for Social Reform, headed by the distinguished Prussian civil servant Berlepsch, surveyed the situation of waiters who at this time depended almost exclusively on the tips of customers for a living [64]. Another association that specialized in improvement of workers' living quarters circulated a questionnaire in Prussia through the help of a medical journal [6]. It asked for information on all aspects of living conditions, from the extent of humidity and the nature of the floor to the availability of drinking water and toilet facilities. The Association for Private Care in Frankfurt a.M. conducted a series of surveys and investigations on the condition of adopted children. These were analyzed by Othmar Spann who was at the time a researcher for the Association. In a 1906 survey [131] he examined the mortality rates of illegitimate children under various forms of care, and was able to demonstrate that the children adopted by strangers or cared for by their mothers living alone had a higher mortality rate than those cared for by the grandparents or by the mothers living unmarried with the fathers.

From the side of the working class itself, surveys of the level of wages and factory conditions in a given industry were undertaken by trade unions or other workers' associations. The pioneer in this area was the Association of German Woodworkers, no doubt in part due to the enlightened leadership of Theodor Leipart [83]. Some of the trades in the Association, like the carpenters, had a tradition of periodically surveying members on the length of the working week, sickness, unemployment, wages and rents, that dated back to the 1880s. Another example was the Association of German Steelworkers which published a fat volume of statistics based on a 1910 survey of part of its membership [155]. In the introduction to the volume, the nature of the investigation was clearly described: 'Our investigations covered the length of shifts and wages of foundry workers, piece-rate work, overtime, observance of national laws, procedures for dismissal, manner of remuneration, accidents, unsanitary conditions in the factories, penalties, and the sickness- and pensionfunds of the enterprises.' The association intended to use the findings as a check on the enforcement of existing legislation and to press for higher wages and better conditions with the entrepreneurs and the government. While most of these social research activities had a practical value, they did not contribute to the development of social science as such.[2]

2. The autobiographies

The period after 1900 saw the emergence of autobiographies by workers as a new literary form aimed at a wide public and intended to create sympathy for the problems of the underdog. The initiator of the autobiographies was Paul Göhre, who had not remained inactive after his initial success in the Evangelical-Social Congress. Within the Congress he represented the left-wing faction, until in 1899 he parted ways with Naumann over the question of support of the

[2] In the post-war years on the other hand the monumental investigations especially of the Associated Unions of Employees on the socio-economic condition of their membership [51] went far beyond pre-war efforts both in scope and methodological sophistication, and was furthermore incorporated into a body of theory on stratification and social mobility by the work of such sociologists as Theodor Geiger and Svend Riemer.

monarchy and became an active socialist supporter and a social democratic deputy in the Reichstag [63, p. 170]. From 1904 to the war he embarked on a project of publishing autobiographies of workers that captured the public's attention and soon found a number of imitators. Göhre intended to prove to the privileged classes that the working man's misery was man created and could therefore be changed by man. He wanted to acquaint them with the drab setting and prospects of working class life, and to prove them that the working man too had human thoughts and feelings, and reacted to joy and suffering in the same way they did. Lack of knowledge about the lower class was especially widespread in Germany where the social novel in the tradition of Victor Hugo, Charles Dickens, and Emile Zola never attained prominence.[3]

The first book in the Göhre series was that of Karl Fischer in 1904 [48], written in authentic vernacular without chapter headings. For example, Fischer recalled that after several years of working in a brick factory he finally got to see the director as he came by one day with a visitor, and that the director asked him what he was doing. 'So I have at least once seen the director at close quarters and have heard him speak with my own ear...' (p. 355) was his reaction to the brief encounter. His sense of satisfaction and feeling of being honored in being spoken to by the director had a ring of authenticity about it and contradicted the stereotype of resentment at the entrepreneur. What made Fischer's book so moving was the picture of the little man who is being taken advantage of without ever getting a break, which his straightforward narrative recreated admirably. Karl Fischer's recollections were followed up by those of other workers, Moritz Bromme in 1905, F. L. Fischer in 1906, Wenzel Holek in 1909 and Franz Rehbein in 1911, all edited by Göhre. Others now joined in to make this new literary genre widespread. Adolf Levenstein in 1909 created quite a sensation in editing a pair of volumes of essays and poems by

---

[3] When Göhre's account of factory life [52] appeared back in 1891, a conservative newspaper admitted that 'we were better acquainted with the condition of life of the half savage African tribes than with those of our own people' [109, p. 10]. An interesting American parallel to Göhre's factory experiences and the implicit challenge it presented to the prevalent Darwinian mood were the experiences of Whiting Williams, personnel director of a business firm. In 1919 he decided to get to know the workers from direct contact and 'put on overalls to find out.' Upon summing up his life as a worker in *What's in the Worker's Mind* [173] he wrote (p. 281): 'Certainly the most outstanding impression of all is that I found my companions in the labor gangs and mines so completely human and so surprisingly normal.'

workers entitled *From the Depths* [86] and *Worker-Philosophers and Poets* [87]. He also organized an exposition of workers' paintings in Berlin. Levenstein had assembled these materials in a roundabout way by corresponding with the more literate and artistic respondents of an attitude survey which he published only later in 1912 (see section 7). The greatest success, however, of all the autobiographies was obtained by that of the leading Austrian socialist woman Adelheid Popp in 1909 [109]. The English translation of her book contained introductions by both August Bebel and Ramsey MacDonald. It was the moving story of a girl with a widowed mother, who had to contribute to the family's support at an early age while suffering from chronic mental disorders. She developed a passion for reading historical novels which were her only escape from drab reality. She slowly discovered her gift for public speaking and organization, and through a friend of her brother was converted to the socialist cause. Her story confirmed a point already noted by Göhre about the effectiveness of personal contact in bringing about political awareness. Before her conversion she was so engrossed in the world of duchesses and princes through her readings that she was an enthusiastic supporter of the emperor and did not link her own hardships to the established social order. A few years later she wrote another book of recollections.[4]

3. *The monographs*

A systematic monograph on the reading habits of workers was published in 1910 by the librarian Walter Hofmann [67] after he had kept a

---

[4] The curious thing about these workers' memoirs was that they were generally ignored by the students of socialism and the working class until after WW I. To be sure it was fashionable to include a brief chapter on worker-psychology in any scholarly book on the working class question and to refer in passing to the autobiographies, even to insert a quote from one of the Levenstein poems at the head of the chapter title. After the war they became an important topic in their own right and tended to be overvalued as a source of information about the lower class mentality. Eugen Rosenstock in 1922 illustrated his theories of industrial work by focusing entirely on the autobiography of the worker Eugen May [96]. Robert Michels was less arbitrary in his *Psychology of Anti-Capitalist Movements* [99] in that he cited a lot of them, both German and foreign. Michels was somewhat influenced by the theories of the social darwinists. He saw in the autobiographies evidence that the workers were less apt to possess the gift of rational thinking (pp. 271-274). A dissertation by Koch [77] written under Michels remained the only systematic attempt to analyze the autobiographies as documents with sociological value and to compare them with other sources such as Levenstein's attitude survey and Göhre's participant observation method.

careful record of the books taken out from a public library in Dresden and the background of its readers, over a two-year period. He was inspired to do this study after reading several autobiographies of workers (p. 239). His intention was to compare the mentality of the two classes through the kinds of books they were in the habit of reading. Hofmann classified the readers according to their occupations into five groups, two of them adult, the first with 1,372 members he called 'the proletarians,' the second with 881 members on record were the 'bourgeois'. So as not to bias his findings, he excluded from the 'bourgeois' category people in the academic professions because of their specialized and vocational reading needs. He actually presented over 50 pages of tables of findings. His first procedure was to draw up a list of most-read books, then for each title give the percent of readers in the proletarian category, percent of readers in the bourgeois category. Then he examined types of literature read in great detail, by dividing all books taken out into several such categories as Belles Lettres, Historical Novels, Fiction, Mysteries, Travel, etc., and further subdividing these categories – for Belles Lettres he had Ancient Classical, Ancient German, German Romantic, Classical Dramas, etc. Then within these subdivisions he listed titles of books taken out and the frequency of both proletarian and bourgeois readers. He also kept an extensive record of 50 readers over a 3-1/2 year period, and noted down every book they had taken out, as well as their age and occupation.

Hofmann's records might be questioned on several points, the most obvious one being that there is no assurance a book taken out was read, at least in its entirety, and that if the 'bourgeois' readers did not take out some books this might be because they owned a copy of it at home. But there can be no question that he pioneered an entirely novel area of research based on institutional records. Hofmann had difficulty in summarizing his data into a presentable and usable form. It may be of historical interest to present at least a few findings. Thus the average number of books taken out in two years was 28.23 for the bourgeois readers and 22.68 for the proletarians; on the other hand 40.7 per cent of the books read by proletarians were classified as scientific literature, as opposed to 35.46 percent for the bourgeois readers [p. 291, Table I]. If one examines the list of most popular novelists, one is struck by the similar rank order of preference of the two classes as well as their predilection for foreign writers. Jules Verne,

Dumas, Walter Scott, Zola, Dickens and Maupassant are the most read authors, Goethe and Schiller are far behind. The favorite German author was Hauptmann, and he was less popular than Mark Twain for example.

Another interesting monograph on a limited topic, but treated in depth, was the 1912 study of three generations of Krupp workers by Ehrenberg and his assistant Racine [36]. Ehrenberg was a professor of economics at Rostock opposed to the dominant historical school of economics and their grand theories of stages of economic development. Ehrenberg drew his inspiration from the early 19th century economist Thünen and his analytic and quantitative treatment of socio-economic processes. In order to establish exact mobility rates and test hypotheses about its determinants Ehrenberg chose 692 employees at Krupp who had been with the firm for 30 or more years at the end of 1906. Since almost 200 of them already had their fathers working for Krupp and most of them had a grown-up son at work, Ehrenberg was able to span three generations for a good part of his sample. The data on each family was obtained by direct interviews from the workers themselves and from the files of Krupp, and dealt with the exact occupational history, earnings, illnesses, savings, education, and family of the employees. Ehrenberg was, of course, aware that his sample was not representative of Krupp employees as a whole because of their long time employment with Krupp, their higher average income and their occupational distribution (pp. 26-31). He was, however, willing to sacrifice this criterion in favor of obtaining precise data. The analysis of occupational and social mobility carried out by Ehrenberg on the basis of these data represents a sophisticated approach to the subject.

The monograph was divided into two parts. The first part consisted of a detailed analysis of the 196 families for whom data on three generations was available. For each family a two-page abstract was presented, including a graph of its average yearly income from the 1860s to 1906 and a separate plot of the average earning of all Krupp employees for comparison. In the margin of the graph major events such as illness, retirement, and job changes were indicated. From these 'family monographs' Ehrenberg distinguished 20 overall patterns: for each generation, the situation of the family could be 'especially favorable,' 'favorable,' 'average' or 'below average,' depending upon its level of income as compared to the average income of all Krupp employees in the relevant years. The mobility pattern of a family would then be characterized by the sequence of family situations in all three generations.[5] Ehrenberg made a careful, though impressionistic, analysis of the reasons why one family might show a predominantly upward mobility sequence, yet one quite like it in the first generation might not.

The second part of the monograph was a numerical re-analysis of the pooled data for all the employees in his sample. Among the findings which Ehrenberg was able to demonstrate in tables or graphs, one clearly showed (p. 340) that white collar earnings rose much faster than blue collar earnings in the years 1877-1905, though in 1877 the initial average income for both sets of occupations was roughly equal. Moreover (p. 342) the white collar income showed a steady upward rise whereas the blue collar income was subject to the fluctuations of the good and bad years of the business cycle. As to inter-generational findings, Ehrenberg showed (p. 353) that there was no occupational mobility difference in the second generation between those whose fathers had been on the one hand either in the trades, independent farming or clerical work and on the other hand in skilled factory work or minig. At the same time the total life income of the second generation tended to be higher in the *same* occupations for those whose fathers had been in the trades, etc., than for those whose fathers had been skilled workers. As to the descendants of unskilled workers and agricultural laborers, both their occupational mobility and total life earnings (even in the same occupations) were lower than that of the first two groups.[6] As to the influence of the second generation occupation and lifetime income upon the occupation or occupational choice of the third generation, white collar fathers or skilled workers with above average income were able to send a far higher proportion of their sons into white collar, sales, technical and other jobs with an educational prerequisite.[7] Besides these interesting findings Ehrenberg took

[5] There are $3^4 = 81$ possible different patterns, but because of the nature of the original sample most of the predominantly downward-mobile patterns were not represented.
[6] Ehrenberg's own analysis of the table (p. 353) on the influence of father's occupation upon son's occupation and overall life-income is not quite correct. The format of table itself is on the other hand more sophisticated than the usual father-son occupation tables in current mobility studies.
[7] To classify a person according to whether his average life income is below or above the average life income of the people in his occupation is to make use of a property of the collectivity to which he belongs. This procedure is just currently getting widespread attention in social research in connection with contextual analysis.

upon himself to establish the relationship of many other factors to mobility. Some of these were of an age to entry into the labor market, nature
of the first job, the number of brothers and sisters, the savings of parents,
the type of parental housing, parents' health, etc., but because of the
nature of his data, the limited number of cases he was working with and
the many interrelations between these factors, the results achieved were
inconclusive. [8]

Ehrenberg did demonstrate for the first time that there had been
considerable upward occupational mobility for some factory workers
at least, and that the prospects for their children appeared even more
hopeful. His work was however completely ignored by other economists.

The way in which scientific issues, to their detriment, were often
embroiled in conflicts of ambitions and personalities is perhaps best
illustrated in the case of Ehrenberg. He had started rather late upon
an academic career after having been a businessman. He openly
favored economic liberalism and *laisser-faire* and attacked the 'socialists
of the chair' at business conventions. They in turn looked upon him
as a mere spokesman for the business interests totally lacking in
intellectual integrity. They also resented his claim of being an
innovator in quantitative and analytic methods in economics. Ehrenberg was no doubt an ambitious man and would have preferred the
prestige of a Leipzig professorship to the relative obscurity of Rostock.
When he approached Bücher, the leading Leipzig economist, in order
to secure an appointment there, he was snubbed. Subsequently when
in 1908 some businessmen approached the university at Leipzig with
the intention of endowing a professorial chair provided that Ehrenberg
were called to take it, he became ostracized and his scientific work
completely ignored. Thereupon Ehrenberg founded and edited an
economic journal, the *Thünen Archiv* (later called the *Archiv für exakte
Wirtschaftsforschung*), which was boycotted to the extent that only he and
his assistants published in it for lack of papers submitted by other
economists. Ehrenberg also planned setting up an Institute for
Economic Research [37], modelled after natural science institutes,
where data from business firms and households would be analyzed.
The Institute would provide valuable experience and support for
students writing dissertations, and the more gifted and experienced

[8]   Progress on how to combine this sort of information to study its impact upon
mobility has yet to be made.

students would become permanent research associates of the institute. Ehrenberg thus intended to fill a void in research which existed between the activites of the university seminars on the one hand, and those pursued in the government statistical bureaus on the other. For both the raw data and the financial support of the undertaking (estimated at 40,000 Marks yearly), Ehrenberg saw the need for seeking support from the business community. These efforts were in turn denounced by his opponents as an effort to further his own career and as additional proof of his subservience to business interests. Yet who could deny the real need for detailed empirical studies of economic action and for research institutes. Many social scientists including Weber and Tönnies quite independently of each other came to the same conclusion and made efforts to secure funds for social research institutes.

Another area of social life which was empirically studied on a modest scale for the first time is described in Emilie Altenloh's *Sociology of the Movies* [4], part of a series on contemporary cultural life under the editorship of Alfred Weber. Altenloh set out to explore the relationship between social class and entertainment and cultural pursuit. She distributed a short questionnaire (p. 2) to lower class audiences which was quite condescending in tone. Question #6 for example read: 'Whatever induces you to go to a movie?'; #8: 'Do you stay for the entire length of the performance?'; and #11; 'Have the movies communicated to you any artistic impressions?' Altenloh did not bother to present and findings in tabular or numerical form. She used her data to illustrate the preconceived notions she entertained on the effects of seeing blood and violence upon an audience bent on cheap entertainment.

4. *Election studies*

By the turn of the century some newspapers were publishing election analyses based on the data supplied by the statistical bureaus after national elections. More scholarly analysis using ecological correlation also appeared in some journals at this time. That of Adolf Braun [21] in 1903 was still rather descriptive and suffered from a fragmented presentation of the results. But a year later Blank published an election study in the *Archiv für Sozialwissenschaft und Sozialpolitik* entitled

'The social composition of the social-democratic voters in Germany' [15], which combined a sophisticated treatment of ecological data with hypotheses about electoral behavior. Blank noted that in the national elections of 1903 the number of social-democratic votes cast, 3,010,771, exceeded the estimated number of eligible industrial working class voters in the population, 2,446,000. To arrive at the latter figure (pp. 515-520) Blank extrapolated the number of industrial workers from the 1895 figures, the last census count available, made allowances for the non-voters, excluded foreign workers and those without a fixed residence or under the eligible age of 25. This procedure enabled him to estimate at 564,000 the minimum number of non-working class votes cast for the Social-Democrats, or more than a sixth of the total vote for the party. Blank's ecological analysis consisted of calculating for each state and major city the percentage of industrial workers in its voting population, the percentage of Social-Democratic votes of all votes cast and the percentage of Catholics in the population. He was able to point to a strong negative relationship between Catholicism and socialist support, even in highly industrial Catholic areas (pp. 512-513). He also estimated that in most big cities middle-class elements contributed as much as a third, at times even one half, of the Social-Democratic votes (pp. 527-529). He concluded that the German Social Democratic Party was (p. 539) 'according to its electoral composition not a class party,' and that consequently it would not be able to keep its class character in the long run.[9]

Interest in political affairs also led to studies of the social com-position of the Reichstag, although the most complete and valuable investigations were made in the post-war period. Willy Kremer's dissertation [80] in 1934 examined the occupational background of the

---

[9]   Max Weber, editor of the *Archiv*, wrote a four-page comment (pp. 550-553) following Blank in which he called attention to the importance of voting studies. The next step, Weber wrote, would be to study 'the influence of the non-proletarian element upon the inner nature of the party and the political position due to it,' and the relationship between the 'organized nucleus' of the party and the masses supporting it by votes. But Weber pointed out how difficult it would be for an uncommitted social scientist to have access to party records indispensable for such a study. Robert Michels did subsequently follow up these suggestions. Weber interestingly enough did not single out another perplexing issue raised by Blank's findings, namely the reasons why some middle-class voters supported in such numbers a socialist working class party. It is precisely the opposite phenomenon, namely why in post-war Austria the socialist party did not receive adequate middle-class support, which awakened Lazarsfeld's interest in voting decisions and which ultimately led to the Columbia tradition of voting studies.

Reichstag deputies for each political party and faction between 1871 and 1912. It is indicative of trends in social research that a year earlier another dissertation by Adolf Borell [18] on the composition of the Reichstag used essentially the same data and similar methods quite independently of Kremer.

5. *Elite studies*

The elite and genealogical studies made during the period after 1900 in Germany were inspired by Galton's work on hereditary genius, Fahlbeck's genealogical research on the Swedish aristocracy, and de Candolle's and Odin's studies of the French intellectual and scientific elite. The aim was to trace the social origins of the elites and to try to draw relevant conclusions on the relative importance of heredity and environment in the production of the intellectually gifted. Some of the findings were unfortunately artifacts due to the manner of selecting samples and the retrospective method employed. If one compares the average number of children of a group of people with the average number of children in their parents' families, one will invariably be able to point out a higher average in the previous generation and thus find confirmation for the degeneration hypothesis, because bachelors and marriages without children are included in the present generation and necessarily excluded from the previous generation. In addition because more children might yet be born to the families selected, one further under-represents the number of offspring in the present generation. Only a random sample at both points in time can settle the issue involved here. The methodology of genealogical studies is complicated. One must use extreme care because the failures and less successful branches of a family will usually be more difficult to trace, if at all. Thus the elite and occupational continuities will be highlighted beyond their true proportion, and the discontinuities (produced presumably by the same hereditary configurations) underrated.

Steinmetz [133], from whom Tönnies was to borrow the term 'sociography,' tested in 1904 the degeneration hypothesis on the Dutch elite. He sent questionnaires to the 800 most prominent men in the universities, the arts, the professions, the government, commerce and industry, inquiring about the number of children, their parents' families and their own, their age, education, occupation, etc. The retrospective method he used made for a confirmation of the hypothesis and seemed to show that elite families were less productive of children than their parents had been. In 1908 Ziermer [179], in a genealogical study persued 300 years into the past, tested the hypothesis of inheritance of intellectual abilities on 15 families of the small village Waldau. He spent six years of research tracing in village records, archives and family chronicles the occupations and fates of all branches of these families. The amount of data assembled, the effort expended and the completeness aimed at were in themselves a remarkable achievement. He showed, for example, that the Tanner family, though of lesser means than some of its neighbors, was consistently more productive of artists, ministers and other professionals, and that those of its family members who migrated to cities also fared well. Though Ziermer realized that family tradition and milieu might in part account for these findings, he saw in them a confirmation of the inheritance hypothesis.

In 1915 Otto Most [101] published a study of the economic and social condition of the higher civil service in Prussia. He demonstrated how in absolute terms their salaries had risen less than the cost of living, and in relative terms how their share of the increased standard of life since the 1870s was less than that of the commercial and industrial elite. The consequences were frugal living and fewer children in the civil service families, indicating a weakening of this historically so prominent stratum of the population, and for the country as a whole, a loss of talent into business occupations since government service was so demanding unless one had independent family wealth. A questionnaire survey of 500 higher civil servants on their families supplemented the study, but Most's attempt to show how the impoverishment of the civil servants led to a smaller number of children and a delay in the age of marriage suffered from the lack of a comparable non-civil service control group. Again the retrospective method used to demonstrate the decrease in family size with respect to the previous generation and the lower degree of occupational continuity for government service of their children had the consequence of substantiating the trend that Most wished to illustrate in a more dramatic fashion than was probably actually the case.

The most complete elite study in these years was that of Maas [93] in 1915. It too was inspired by the heredity versus environment controversy and the elite studies of Galton and Odin. Maas chose 4,421 prominent men born after 1700 from the *Allgemeine Deutsche Biographie*, classified them into 17 occupational categories and three broader groups, the intellectual, artistic and practical realms, and investigated trends in the social origin of prominent men as well as the degree of occupational continuity between father and son. It was a sophisticated study in many respects. Maas distinguished between the case of ordinary occupational continuity, 38.7 percent of his sample, and the case of both father and son being prominent in the same occupation, 4.9 percent for the sample.[10] He was able to show that the contribution of the lower social strata to the production of prominent military men, statesmen, jurists, and scientists in the biological and earth sciences, was below their relative contribution to the elite as a whole, whereas their relative contribution of prominent painters, educators and natural scientists exceeded that figure. Most interesting were the tables (pp. 174 ff.) which indicated the trends in the social origin of prominent men born in the three periods 1700-1759, 1759-1818, 1818-1860. These indicated that in the artistic realm, famous artists came increasingly from an artist family background; in the intellectual realm the trend pointed to a decreasing contribution of clergymen, civil service and lower class families in the production of famous scientists and intellectually prominent men, whereas the sons of teachers, doctors, and lawyers correspondingly increased; finally there was a slight drop in the origin of the practical elite from civil service, military and landowner strata, although even in the most recent period of 1818-1860 the three of them contributed over half of all men prominent in the practical realm. One should exercise caution in the interpretation of these trends, however, for they were based on the shifting percentage distribution of the family background of prominent men, and not on rates calculated from the occupational distribution of the population which was unknown.

The study of the military elite in particular was also undertaken in the period before the war. An example was the book of Bleibtreu [16] on the army in 1910, part of the series *Die Gesellschaft* under the editorship of Martin Buber, which aimed at a popular yet not popularized treatment of social topics and issues, and to which men like

---

[10] For single occupations music was the highest with 8.7 percent of both father and son among the famous artists.

Tönnies, Simmel, Sombart, Bernstein, Oppenheimer, Brinkmann and Hellpach also contributed, to name but a few of the better known authors. A quantitative analysis of the social origin of the German officer corps was developed further after the war. We single out only the book of Demeter [33] in 1935.

6. *Higher education*

The Germans were rightly proud of their higher educational system which the United States used as a model when it started to expand and revise its higher education. They also had a long tradition of concern and precise research of their institutions of higher learning. The early 19th century directors of the Prussian Statistical Agency, Hofmann and Dieterici, and their successors Engel and von Mayr, all wrote monographs on the statistics of higher education and established the collection of educational and school statistics as a responsibility of the statistical agencies. From 1891 *Minerva, Yearbook of the Learned World* was published in Germany, and it contained a listing of all professors at all the universities in the world, divided by country, institution of higher learning and faculties, as well as useful information on the universities themselves. This tradition also produced some outstanding studies of educational trends which combined and rounded out a cultural-historical approach with quantitative analysis. In 1884 Conrad published a 250-page monograph entitled 'The attendance at universities in Germany during the last 50 years, with special reference to Prussia' [30]. In the introduction (p. 1) Conrad pointed out the importance of the universities for the cultural development of Germany and the need for a precise statistical representation of the facts, and then added that 'the cultural historian has the right to complement the statistician and on the basis of these numbers, as well as by taking into account the total cultural and economic setting, to clothe this skeleton and to create a complete cultural picture.' Conrad himself tabulated both the absolute number of students and the rate per 100,000 inhabitants in universities in Prussia yearly since 1831-32. He examined the fluctuations in these rates, analyzed the figures separatley by the various faculties, the geographical and social origin of the students, the duration of university attendance. Conrad also pursued some specific issues in more concrete fashion. For his own university of Halle, he selected (pp. 48 ff.) six periods of four years each between 1768 and 1881 and analyzed the trend of the social and occupational background of the students in the faculties of the university. He also examined (p. 138) the trend of the distribution of students within the philosophical faculty by major field of study. In his conclusion Conrad called attention to a recent drop in the number of lawyers, doctors and ministers per 100,000 inhabitants despite the steady increase in the number of students pursuing higher education.

In the following generation it was Franz Eulenburg who continued Conrad's work on university education. In a study of over 300 pages entitled 'The attendance at German universities from the time of their foundation to the present' [44] he established by meticulous research from 'over a million and a half entries of students in university records' as well as by extrapolation and estimation procedures the total number of students attending each university each year since their foundation in the Middle Ages. He also tried to trace trends in the social composition of the student bodies, the shifting length of the study years, the distribution of students among the faculties and prospective occupations, etc. The purpose of these investigations was clearly indicated at the start and pointed to a continuity with Conrad's work (p. 6): 'Through these researches we have the opportunity to establish quantitatively and to measure certain complex manifestations in the area of cultural life... We can make the attempt here on the example of a single concrete case to pursue the distribution of students among the faculties and their choice of study and to draw from them certain conclusions on the dominant values and the intellectual climate of the times. It is evidently not a chance occurrence that in a given period theological studies, or legal studies, or medical and scientific studies are being pursued to a greater degree. Such occurrences can to some degree be the expression of deeper underlying trends. The task here will be to point out definite regularities.' Eulenburg's analysis of the quantitative trends showed that such events as the Thirty Years War and the Napoleonic Wars were marked by a sharp drop in the registration figures. He also showed how the preeminence of certain universities in the early period was related to their geographical position in the trade routes network which affected the overall prosperity of the cities. The presence of prominent professors, intellectual and social currents, and the political fate of the states in which the universities were located also left their imprint upon the statistical data.[11]

Eulenburg was also a keen student of contemporary German higher education. It is most unfortunate and quite indicative of the pre-war German academic milieu that his objective investigations should become the occasion for bitter controversy and polemics with the consequence of blocking his professorial appointment for 18 years [13, p. 247]. Already in 1903 Eulenburg [45] systematically analyzed the age distribution of professors by universities and faculties separately, and pointed to the need for a fixed retirement age at 65 or 70. But it was his frank advocacy of reform in the renumeration of the *Privatdozenten* at the first German Conference of University Teachers in 1908, where he was asked to fill in as speaker in the absence of Friedrich Paulsen, which brought down on his head the ire of some of the older and better known professors, notably Brentano [23, pp. 286 ff.], and which had a deplorable effect upon his subsequent career. Eulenburg [46] had carried out in preparation of his speech a questionnaire survey of university teachers at all levels, to inquire about their salaries, course loads, the number of dissertations supervised, etc., which had met with widespread resentment but enabled him to demonstrate that while the *Privatdozenten*, the lowest ranking university teachers, carried a large part of the entire teaching load, the consequence of not paying them a fixed salary was to prevent the more able and diligent young men from entering an academic career in favor of those with an independent source of wealth.[12]

7. Adolf Levenstein's attitude survey

None of the accomplishments of these years can compare in scope with Adolf Levenstein's attitude survey which was finally published in

[11]   An exhaustive analysis by a single man could, however, not do full justice to the prodigious amount of data assembled by Eulenburg. He himself was helped in the tabulating and computing work by the students in his statistical seminar at Leipzig. The length of his time series, for some universities his figures go back some 400 years continuously, are an unparalleled example of exact information in the area of social and cultural history.

[12]   In 1919 in his famous speech 'Science as a Vocation.' Max Weber stated in a similar critical vein that [169, p. 129] 'the career of an academic man in Germany was generally based on plutocratic prerequisites.'

1912 as *The Working Class Question* [88]. It illustrates once more the extent to which at the start of a new science an outsider and dilettante can be a true innovator and far more successful than the professionals. Levenstein burned with an intense desire to present to the world the living thoughts and hopes of his fellow workers. For years before he hit upon the idea of a questionnaire survey he had held weekly discussions with fellow workers. Then from 1907 to 1911 he sent out 8,000 questionnaires to three categories of workers – miners, steelworkers and textile workers – in eight industrial locations, 1,000 questionnaires intended for each location.[13] He first sent a number of questionnaires to his many friends and contacts, then corresponded and sent other questionnaires to be distributed by those who returned them to him. He thus achieved an extremely high rate of return (63%) which might have been higher still had not the socialist press condemned his undertaking midway through for reasons that are not clear.[14]

Levenstein at first published only essays [86] and poems [87] of some of his more literate friends and respondents, but did show the questionnaires to some professors, including Max Weber, who made vain attempts to convince Levenstein to let some of their students collaborate in a further analysis of the survey. After oral persuasion had failed Weber published a brief article in 1909 entitled *On the Methodology of Socialpsychological Surveys and on Their Analysis* [165] in which he publicly called upon Levenstein to undertake a numerical analysis of his data while at the same time giving him advice on how to do it. Apparently this form of pressure had its effect though Levenstein did not follow all the advice and categorically refused to have his coding and tabulating checked by university students and professors [62, p. 700].

The Levenstein questionnaire explored the workers' attitudes on all the burning issues of the day. Even though the questions were phrased in clumsy fashion, and sometimes quite different items were lumped into the same question (cf. questions ≠19, 22, 24), they covered a wide slice of the workers' motivation, satisfaction, aspirations and general attitude toward their situation in life. The questionnaire was

---

[13] Weber mentioned [165, p. 950] an even earlier 1905 questionnaire survey by Levenstein on workers' attitudes towards a general strike. Levenstein himself did not refer to it and its results were never published.
[14] Herkner hypothesized [62, p. 700] that it was because Levenstein belonged to an anarchist group, but there is no hard evidence for that.

later divided by Levenstein into five sections for purpose of analysis. The first section, questions #1-8, was background data such as name, age, occupation, marital status, number of children, income, manner of payment, and length of the work day. Weber in his critique [165, pp. 950-951] suggested that more background data was needed, such as place of birth, religion, father's occupation, and a detailed job history. The second section, questions #9-13, 16-18, 20, dealt with such matters as fatigue, monotony, preference for piece rates or hourly wages, thoughts during work and other topics which also became important for the Verein für Sozialpolitik survey of factory workers. The second section ended with the loaded question #20: 'What depresses you more, the low level of pay, or that you are so dependent upon the employer, that you have such limited prospects to advance in life, that you have nothing to offer to your children?'[15] The third section, with questions #10, 11, 14, 15 and 26, dealt with hopes and wishes, preferred hours of work, what the worker would do if he had enough spare time, what he would buy if he had enough money, and what occupation he would choose if given the opportunity. The remaining two sections were on cultural and political matters such as reading, political interests, belief in God, and included the topical question #19 on drinking that antagonized a lot of respondents. Question #25: 'Do you go often into the forest? What do you think of when you lie on the ground, and everything is still and quiet all around?' which Weber thought was 'grotesque' actually turned out to be an interesting projection question for those who answered it.

Now the difficulty with open-ended, unstructured questions of the kind that Levenstein asked is that they will be answered on different dimensions by different people. If one asks people what they dislike about their jobs, a certain proportion will answer that pay is not sufficient while others will not like the monotony of work or the chances of advancement. On the other hand it may be still true that among those who find their work too monotonous, many are dissatisfied with the pay, and among those who complain about pay, many would say their job is monotonous if they were specifically asked. Today one would first ask the workers a very general question, such as: 'On

---

[15] Note a similarly loaded pair of questions in Marx's 1880 questionnaire [20, p. 207], #26 and #27: 'In case of accident, is the employer obliged by law to pay compensation to those who have met with an accident while working to enrich him? If not, has he even paid compensation to those who have met with an accident while working to enrich him?'

the whole, are you very satisfied, satisfied, indifferent, dissatisfied or very dissatisfied with your job,' followed by another question enumerating a whole list of items including pay, monotony, and advancement, and have the respondents check off those items they had complaints about. Furthermore there would have to be another follow-up question on the saliency of each complaint, either asking the respondent after each item how important it is to him, or alternatively asking him to list his complaints in order of decreasing importance to him. Levenstein's results are useful for purposes of comparison among the various groups of workers, although no statement can be made about the absolute proportion of workers in the various groups who did have a specific complaint. Thus one might check whether or not among the lowest paid workers and for those with many children a greater proportion spontaneously mention the level of pay as inadequate, or whether such complaints are generally diffused throughout the workers regardless of number of children and income level, which would then indicate that this complaint is a general indicator of dissatisfaction and would require further analysis to be explained.

Levenstein's Questionnaire

Dear Friend, a great favor is asked of you. I would like to know something about your feelings and thoughts, how the work affects you, which hopes and desires you have. Surely you will find a quiet hour to fill out the enclosed questions. We ask the same of your wife. Write from the bottom of your soul. No names will be mentioned. Many thanks.

1. Name.
2. Age.
3. Occupation.
4. Marital Status.
5. How many children do you have?
6. Average weekly earnings.
7. How many hours do you work daily?
8. Do you work for piecerates or for hourly wages and why?
9. Which do you prefer, piecerates or hourly wages, and why?
10. How many hours work would you perform gladly?
11. What would you do if you had enough time daily left to yourself?
12. Do you work with machines, and what kinds of machines are they?
13. Do you experience pleasure in your work, or do you have no interest in it?
14. What kinds of things would you buy if you had enough money?
15. What type of work would you prefer to engage in?
16. Do you always work at the same thing or at different things?

17. Do you feel some sort of tiredness or other hardships from always doing the same type of work?
18. Do you think during work and what are your thoughts, or is it impossible for you to think (while working)?
19. Do you get a greater pleasure out of your family or out of going to the tavern, and do you think that the consumption of alcohol is dispensable, or can you work better after having had a drink?
20. What depresses you more, the low level of pay, or that you are so dependent upon the employer, that you have such limited prospects to advance in life, that you have nothing to offer to your children?
21. What books have you read?
22. What influence do the political and trade union movements exercise upon you.
    Do you hope that through them things will become better for you?
23. Or are you without hope, and why?
24. Do you believe in God, or have you left the established church, and why?
25. Do you go often into the forest?
    What do you think of when you lie on the ground, and everything is still and quiet all around?
26. What hopes and wishes do you have?

Before some of the results are presented here, a word remains to be said about Levenstein's manner of analysis and Weber's advice to him. Levenstein presented the results separately for each question and each of the three main categories of workers. He would quote some two dozen answers directly, specifying in the margin the respondents' age, average pay, number of children, and whether or not the answer quoted was typical. Next he would present tables of the kinds of answers, sometimes controlled for age, and sometimes for average pay, whereas Weber had advised him to control for both variables simultaneously (165, pp. 954-5]. Following Weber's advice he included however the coding categories 'no answer' and 'other,' but he percentaged most tables in the wrong direction.[16] Finally Levenstein would summarize the findings for the question by presenting the marginal frequencies for each of the main groups of workers, but would not offer a verbal interpretation based on the inspection of the figures and the tables.

[16] Weber did not suggest two procedures that are often used by present day survey researchers with the type of questions Levenstein asked. The first is multiple coding; the second is crosstabulating the answers to two attitude questions or to parts of the same question, in addition to crosstabulating attitudes with background variables. For example one would today crosstabulate respondents on their 'hopes' and 'wishes' from question 26.

Levenstein was also aware that a mere reproduction of the answers question after question was not enough, but that a common element was manifest in the same respondent's answers to all the questions. This common element stood as a mark of his basic character. Levenstein coped with the problem by improvising a typology of workers' mentality consisting of four categories. At the top was the elite of the working class, 5.9% strong, the 'intellectual' stratum. It was made up of 'creative, autonomous individuals' filled with 'youthful optimism'. Next, with 9.9% of the workers, came the 'contemplative' stratum consisting of the 'lonely' and the 'misunderstood'. A third and more sizable group with 20.1% of the respondents was the 'pretentious' stratum of workers who gave wordy and pseudo-intellectual answers, and cited from books they did not understand. The remaining 64.1% Levenstein called the 'mass' stratum, the stratum of the 'spiritually dead'. They gave mostly brief yes and no, or even obscene, answers to the questions. It is clear, however, from Levenstein's own examples that he did not follow any systematic procedure in deriving the four strata and in classifying the respondents into them. From the quotes of workers it is evident that a sizable group gave quite religious and tradition oriented answers to some of the questions, and these respondents were merely lumped into either the 'pretentious' or 'mass' stratum.[17] Weber was extremely critical of Levenstein's intuitive approach to typology building, but as it turned out was unable to sway him on this point. While Weber did not suggest a specific typology to Levenstein, his thinking on empirical typology construction had a very modern ring to it and differed from the ideal type constructions of his theoretical and historical analyses. It deserves to be quoted in full [165, p. 956]: 'Only then, after the material has been quantitatively exploited and various parts of it brought into relationship with each other, only then might one try to construct on the basis of this foundation types of proletarian mentality and awareness, formal as well as substantive types.... At any rate one must further proceed on the basis of numbers to tackle this problem, that is to say investigate certain differences in the frequency of certain styles of expression and of thought-orien-

---

[17] The curious thing about the typology was that Levenstein did not make any use of it in the analysis. Ordinarily one builds types from some questions to be able to point to differences in answer on other questions and to explain these differences from the types. This Levenstein did not do.

tation by age, income, and place of origin of the respondents; dubious
cases should be excluded, while the clearcut ones, if that seems possible
carefully brought together into types (and also combinations of types
and transitional types), all this (should be done) however very carefully,
and with constant re-examination of the original data.' This passage
would indicate that Weber favored a quantitative approach to typology building from qualitative data. Moreover his notion of arriving
at the 'right' dimensions after constructing provisional 'transitional'
types and 'combinations' of them, is in the spirit of contemporary
typological procedures known as reduction and substruction [81, pp.
40-53].

8. Levenstein's findings

We now turn to the findings and present an interpretation insofar as
that is possible from the crosstabulations in the text and the supporting
data.

First a few differences in the age and income distribution of the
eight categories of workers. By age steel-workers were about five
years older on the average than the textile workers and the miners.
About 50 percent of the respondents of these two groups were between
25 and 35 years of age. Differences in earning were far sharper, and
geographical location as well as type of work was important. The rank
order of the groups by income is indicated in the following table.

Group	Modal income	P.c. in mode	Number of respondents
1. Steelworkers-Berlin	30-40 Marks/week	55.4%	712
2. Miners-Ruhr	20-30 M	48 %	810
3. Textile workers-Berlin	20-30 M	72.8%	419
4. Steelworkers-Solingen	20-30 M	63.5%	696
5. Miners-Saar	20-30 M	84 %	720
6. Textile workers-Forst	10-20 M	56.3%	734
7. Steelworkers-Oberstein	10-20 M	74.5%	395
8. Miners-Schlesien	10-20 M	84.7%	554

Thus the difference between highest and lowest paid group was of the
order of three times as much. Note that the rate of return in the last
column (since 1,000 questionnaires were sent to each location) was
not related to average earnings. Levenstein did not indicate reasons

for the varying rates of return, but the overall rate of 63 percent is an extremely good figure. The sample was not random in the usual sense since Levenstein corresponded with workers who had returned their questionnaire in order to enlist their support for distributing more among their friends and colleagues. But the sheer size of the total response probably ensured that all shades of opinion were represented in it.

The world of work. In question #9 the worker was offered a choice between piece rates and hourly wages. Most workers at this time were doing piece work and this was a considerable source of friction between labor and capital. The answers in all eight groups were from 4:1 to 6:1 in favor of hourly wages. Judging from the direct quotes, the Marxist slogan 'piece work is slave work' must have been the favorite expression on this matter. The reasons given were: more stable income, better for health, for reasons of solidarity, and work less exacting. Among those in favor of piece rates 'higher income' was the main reason given. As one might expect, among the highest paid workers there was less sentiment for hourly wages than among the others, yet among the Ruhr miners the best paid group was 30:1 in favor of hourly wages. The reversal of the relationship in the Ruhr was an interesting result. It was probably an indication of the greater solidarity and class consciousness of the Ruhr miners.

To the question 'How many hours work would you perform gladly?' a vast majority among the textile and steelworkers answered 'eight hours.' This was also the most frequent answer to the question 'After how many hours work do you get tired?' The explanation here seems to be quite simply that the socialist agitation for the eight-hour day was widely supported by the workers at large. Yet here too a reality factor was operating. The relationship between hour at which fatigue sets in and increasing age was quite striking for all groups. Older workers indicated fatigue after fewer hours of work on the average than younger workers. Furthermore the miners tended to get tired after four to six hours and also prefer a work day shorter than eight hours. Levenstein never tabulated the actual hours of work performed, nor did he crosstabulate the actual versus preferred hours of work. The average length of the working day was probably close to ten hours at this time for the type of worker in the survey, less for the miners. From these answers it would then appear that the question

of fatigue was by this time not as crucial as in the earlier days of the
industrial revolution. From the direct quotes of workers' answers, only
the miners were complaining persistently. All the more serious were
the psychological problems associated with factory work. We turn
now to this issue as it was reflected in the answers to some questions
in the survey.

Question #13: 'Do you experience pleasure in your work, or do you
have no interest in it?' drew an overall ratio of 8:1 answers in which
dislikes outweighed the likes. Here, too, there were variations by
average income earned. Among the highest paid the ratio tended to
decrease to 2:1, among the lowest paid textile workers it rose as high
as 12:1 in favor of disliking the job. The actual answers covered a
wide range of reasons which throw considerable light on the psychological processes operating in the workers' minds and deserve docu-
mentation.

A. 33-year-old miner – 'I must like my work because I was born for work.'
B. 26-year-old miner – 'The job gives me no pleasure. I go to work as
I would go to die.'
C. 29-old-year miner – 'I like my work if I make enough money at it.'
D. 47-year-old miner – 'Pleasure? No. But my work becomes interesting
through my hobby, geology....'
E. 39-year-old textileworker – 'I must be interested, my stomach demands
it.'
F. 52-year-old textileworker – 'I like my job if I can return home to my
family on Saturday with a full wallet.'
G. 54-year-old textileworker – 'The work is pleasurable and I am happy
when it turns out neat and beautiful.'
H. 55-year-old textileworker – 'Not pleasurable in present day bourgeois
society.'

Here we have side by side the tradition minded and the rebel, the
alienated and the craftsman taking pride in his product. These answers
were doubtless not the most ordinary ones. Levenstein's code actually
showed that the two most frequent types of answer for disliking one's
job were 'monotony' and 'not enough pay.' Another common type
of answer with about 15 percent response in all groups was 'because
the work helps support the capitalists.' Most of those who answered
the question positively did so because the job payed well or was
versatile.

Question #20, because it was worded so suggestively, was biased to
elicit an ideological answer, yet only about a third of the respondents

answered that 'dependence upon the employer is more painful than low pay.' Even such a biased question showed that a reality factor was present. Among the steelworkers as one went from lower average wages to higher wages, the percent who resented their condition of dependence more than low pay increased regularly from 27 percent for those earning less than 30 M a week, to 35 percent for those making between 30 and 40 M, and finally 65 percent for thoes making more than 40 M a week. For the textile workers and miners this relationship was, however, only slightly positive. Evidence that 'average pay' as a variable made a significant difference in the attitudes of the workers also came in question #18 on the thoughts of the workers during work. Levenstein got criticized for asking this question at all, perhaps with good reason if his intention was to find out what the workers *actually* were thinking about during the job. As a projective device, however, this question was probably successful. Compare the following answers that were reproduced in full:

A. 20-year-old textileworker – 'Sir, I am young. I shall be frank with you, when nothing special is up I think about my girl friend.'

B. 26-year-old miner – 'I think about my family, that I may return home healthy.'

C. 29-year-old miner – 'Impossible to think since I must keep an eye on the mountain to protect my life.'

D. 49-year-old miner – 'Can't think. Can only swear.'

E. 35-year-old miner – 'I think very often during work. When I am really tired the poem occurs to me: "How tired I am, I would like best to lie down in the grave, to sleep eternally. O life, my life, thou bringest me great sorrow."'

To cover the intensity of feelings expressed, the worry in B and C as opposed to the carefree attitude of A and the despair of E, this would be a tough set of answers to code meaningfully. It would have to be coded along several dimensions. Levenstein's own way was actually the easiest solution, though not the most meaningful one. He merely listed the content of the thoughts, such as 'with the family,' 'with the pay,' 'with political questions,' etc. Since he made no cross-tabulations one can only make rough comparisons subject to the ecological fallacy: it would appear that the better paid groups of workers were more likely to report thoughts on 'political and organizational matters' than the poorer paid workers; conversely the poorer ones worried more about pay.

Hopes and wishes. Question #15: 'What type of work would you prefer to engage in?' illustrates the difficulties inherent in an open-ended question. It was undoubtedly meant to elicit specific occupations, yet roughly 20 percent answered 'that work which brings most money.' Others mentioned 'independent' or 'varied' work. Many of the miners answered 'day shift.' A more successful pair of questions were #11 and #14 on what the worker would do if he had time and money, although here Levenstein's code was poor since almost half the answers were coded as 'various' and 'other,' that is in the residual categories. On the other hand a clear pattern emerges with those answers that were captured. For the money question the pattern seemed to confirm Engel's budget law: as average income of group decreased, the percentage who in a group answer 'would like enough to eat' increased. Conversely with increasing income one was more likely to desire 'a little house with a plot of land.' Fully 37 percent of the Berlin steelworkers, the highest paid group, had set their hearts on this petty-bourgeois goal. As for the question on spare time, as average income increased, the percent who answered 'I would educate myself further' also increased. About one in four answered in this manner among the three highest paid groups. Another type of answer which was quite common for all groups was 'devote more time to the family,' and 'go for a walk in nature' (no doubt the equivalent of sports at a time when sports was not yet widespread as a form mass leisure).

The last question, 'What hopes and wishes do you have?' will be reproduced almost in full because it was quite revealing of the mentality of the working class. Despite differences in interpretation of the question, a sufficient number quite clearly thought of it as referring to political and social changes for the society as a whole and not to their own private fortunes alone. Compare for instance these three answers which Levenstein quoted in full and which range from the utopian mentality to the typical ambivalence between party ideology and actual strategy.

22-year-old miner – 'I have only one desire for myself and the rest of mankind. That she be able to partake very soon in the beauty of the world. The world has enough of it to make all mankind happy and peaceful.'

Other utopian wishes were couched in a more religious terminology. Another respondent's answer revealed typical ambivalence:

32-year-old miner – 'My hopes are that next year in the elections the socialists will win and things will get better. My foremost wish is to carry the banner when the war against the capitalists and the Junkers comes, and to mow them down to the last man.'

A more down-to-earth attitude is expressed by a 46-year-old steel-worker when he merely wrote: 'I hope for better conditions of life and a carefree old age.'

One difficulty with the Levenstein tabulation was that he did not use quite the same coding categories for all three types of workers. Yet there was sufficient overlap to present the following tables of aspirations:

Wishes	Miners	Textile Workers	Steel-worker
To earn more money	21 %	28.5%	?
Utopia	12.5%	12.8%	11.2%
Better life for children	11.3%	10.7%	8.2%
Existence worthy of human being	9.5%	11.8%	14.8%
Settle accounts with the capitalists	4.2%	6.5%	7.3%
None	21.5%	2 %	3 %
'Various other' and 'no answer'	19 %	27.7%	55.5%
n =	2,095	1,153	1,803

As elsewhere the money answer was foremost in the mind of the respondents. The surprising fact, however, was the relative similarity in percent distribution of other kinds of wishes. Levenstein unfortunately did not do further breakdowns of this question by age and income as he had done for some of the previous questions.

Hopes	Miners	Textile Workers	Steel-worker
To earn more money	28.5%	38 %	30.5%
Victory of the Social Democrats	21 %	41.5%	24 %
None	12 %	2 %	3 %
'Other' and 'no answer'	38 %	18.5%	42.5%
n =	2,084	1,243	1,803

Note the mistake in the totals for the textile workers.[18] Levenstein

---

[18]   The total is 1,243 in the 'Hopes' table and 1,153 in the 'Wishes' table.

was probably getting rather tired with the labor involved, and undoubtedly put down a hundred where a ten was required, but never bothered to correct his error. This loss of interest is even more evident with the questions 22 and 23 on the influence of the political and trade union movements and hopes attached to their success. As Levenstein coded both parts of these questions together it is not very usable. Yet it is evident that the number of those who expected a gradual improvement of their lot, 'if not for me then for the children,' outnumber those who foresaw no improvement.

On the basis of the set of questions just presented dealing with the expectations and aspirations of workers, it seems fairly safe to say that a vast majority favored the gradualist approach rather than the revolutionary one, and this in spite of the considerable malcontent with work and wages.[19] There was a small hard core of true revolutionaries to be sure, and an even larger group of alienated workers who were withdrawn and filled with despair. But the overall picture which emerges in no way contradicts Michels' and Schumpeter's analysis of the working class movement at the time. The socialist leaders knew that time was in their favor, while the mass organization upon which their strength rested was developing a conservative ideology from within. This mood of the leaders was in general agreement with the predominant tenor of the workers' answers to the Levenstein questions. The Social Democrats had by this time achieved a monopoly of communication with the workers. Over 40 percent of the textile and steelworkers reported reading primarily socialist books and trade union literature in question #21. There existed no serious competition for the political allegiance of the workers on the part of any alternative ideology. The extent to which religion was no longer a factor to be taken into account was reflected in the answers to question #24 on belief in God. Roughly only one out of four workers answered in the affirmative, and from the replies that Levenstein quoted in full it would seem that a fair proportion of those who professed belief in God did not have the Christian idea of the deity in mind.

---

[19]   Weber's impression from looking over the raw data in 1909 was that [165, p. 956] 'this material confirms at least for me the old experience that the manner of perception of the proletarian... is far more *similar* to that of the 'bourgeois' than the *a priori* class theorists think. That divergences in conception due to different material interests are clearly discernible (and that they follow) directly and rationally from them, is of course self-evident.'

9. *Newspaper and public opinion research: story of a failure*

Another question in the history of empirical research concerns the only prevalent mass medium of the day, the newspapers. How is it that despite modest beginnings no public opinion and communication research developed in Germany? Two kinds of concern centered around newspapers in the period before the War. The first was more political and linked the formation of public opinion with the newspapers; the other more cultural and saw in the press an instrument that influenced the quality of mass culture.

Political theorists had for more than a generation written about public opinion and the newspapers. Phrases and chapter headings such as 'the power of the daily press,' 'the effectiveness of the press in manipulating public opinion,' or 'newspaper and culture' were fairly standard in these writings. The history of various newspapers and their role in German history was also well documented. Another body of data available were lists of newspapers and circulation figures compiled by advertising agencies for prospective advertisers. The pioneering article that utilized this source on newspapers was written in 1898 by Hjalmar Schacht [117], who at the time had not yet started his brilliant career in banking. It was for the most part a comparison of the number of newspapers, circulation figures, prices for advertising space, and their frequency of issue in the various states and geographical areas of Germany. But Schacht also computed the number of inhabitants per newspaper, the price of newspapers with different political affiliation, and cross classified newspapers by states and political affiliation. Such a beginning was modest enough, yet it indicated the possibility of utilizing newspaper statistics for political analysis. By the First World War, a veritable avalanche of dissertations had been written utilizing the advertising catalogs as the source data. One of the more lucid ones is that of M. Wittwer [174] who used Schacht's figures to document a trend of the distribution of newspapers by political affiliation between 1989 and 1913. Wittwer also tabulated the distribution of votes and newspapers by political party in the years 1898 and 1912, and could show for example that the social democrats had increased their portion of the electorate from 27 percent to 35 percent, while the percent of social democratic newspapers had risen only from 1.5 percent to 2.2. percent [174, p. 30].

While all this work was based on more or less crude re-analyses of available information and did not go beyond it, others whose concern with the newspapers was cultural did advance as far as a technique of content analysis of the newspaper itself. In 1903 the influential book of Löbl, *Culture and the Press* [91], classified the 'Inner Structure of the Content' by the social functions assigned to the newspapers (p. 44). There was a section for reports which fulfilled the function of disseminating news; the function of discussion and propagandizing was contained in the articles devoted to criticism, opinion and judgment; the function of providing publicity was met by the advertisements. Löbl also mentioned a residual category that consisted of the literary content of the newspaper. He discussed, however, the relative emphasis of these functions by the newspapers in only impressionistic ways.

In 1910 Paul Stoklossa [134] got the idea from an earlier publication of the Frenchman Henry de Noussance [105] to measure quantitatively the content of newspapers by the number of lines devoted to various subject matters. He took 13 Berlin newspapers and 17 provincial newspapers for an entire week in August and computed the percent of lines, first for each paper separately and then pooled by Berlin vs. provincial newspapers, devoted to domestic news, domestic political editorials, foreign news, foreign editorials, and so on through travel, sports, 'crime, accidents and scandals,' to advertisements. Stoklossa actually used the classification of Noussance, which had the advantage of enabling him to compare Berlin and Parisian, German and French provincial papers.[20] Both men were bent on showing that the papers were neglecting their moral obligation of public education and dissemination of cultural material. Noussance had separated 'useful literature' (3.9 percent for Paris) and 'not useful literature' (9.95 percent). Stoklossa called these 'useful information' (1.06 percent in Berlin) and 'entertainment literature' (5.32 percent). Unfortunately neither described the criteria they had used to make this distinction. It is particularly interesting to note what Stoklossa did not follow up on. Noussance felt the need for going beyond just a count of lines to an assessment of the quality of the contents. From the front page of each paper he jotted down a few characteristic words on such topics as the government and the army. He characterized the *Libre Parole*, for example, as follows: 'This ministry of death and ruin... the army, disorganized in cold blood...I, I am, I have, I know, you see, you will

[20] Noussance had actually performed a content analysis of 20 Parisian and 7 provincial papers only for a singly day, the 27th of November 1901.

see, you will note, imagine, listen, remark... one wonders... the army, the Jews, gold, the cosmopolitans, Israel, the country, double cross, treason, abominable, shocking, immoral...,' recreating in this fashion the anti-semitic and pro-army tone set by its editor Drumont.[21] Stoklossa omitted such an attempt altogether. He contented himself with covering newspapers for an entire week rather than just a single day, but did not make any methodological or conceptual advance on the matter of content analysis.

Both articles were widely quoted in many publications on newspapers, yet did not find any imitators. Despite the fact that Max Weber threw his personal prestige behind this type of investigation at the first meeting of the German Sociological Society in 1910, matters remained at a standstill. Weber had outlined a sociology of the press as the first empirical investigation to be undertaken by the Society [166]. In his usual manner he outlined the problem in its historical and comparative perspective, discussed the inner organization and the distribution of power in the newspapers, and also got down to ask some specific questions, and suggested concrete methods of starting the investigation that were in substance akin to content analysis. 'What type of reading do the newspapers accustom men to?... What kinds of mass beliefs and mass hopes are created and destroyed, what kinds of point of view?' (pp. 440-441), these are some of the concrete questions Weber wanted to find an answer to. He suggested that the researchers begin with exploiting the content of the newspapers themselves (p. 441): 'We will have to start with measuring, in a pedestrian way, with the scissors and the compass, how the contents of the newspapers has quantitatively shifted in the course of the last generation, between light literature and editorial, between editorial and news, between what is or is no longer put (into the papers) as news... And from these quantitative investigations we will have to move on to qualitative ones. We will have to pursue the style of presentation of the papers, how the same problems are treated inside and outside the papers, the apparent repression of emotional presentation....' Weber secured funds for a survey of the press, but when for personal reasons he announced in 1912 at the second meeting of the German Sociological Society his withdrawal as head of the project, he could find no one to step into his place and was disenchanted by the lack of coopera-

---

[21] At this time the Dreyfus affair was raging in France.

tion and readiness for empirical work among his colleagues [158, p. 429].

Beyond even the matter of getting down to analyze the actual content of the papers, one can detect a conviction on the part of many about the overwhelming influence of print upon the mind which it never occured to anyone to put to an empirical test. The most influential figure on the topic of newspapers was at this time the economist Karl Bücher who founded in 1915 the first German school and institute for journalism in Leipzig. Bücher himself was an authority on the history of the newspaper, was a champion of freedom of the press, and encouraged contemporary newspaper research among his students, but only in the sense of newspaper statistics. He wrote in a pessimistic tone [28, p. 55]: 'To calculate the total number of people who regularly read the papers is impossible because we don't even know how many copies are read in common by several families.' It did not occur to him that this was a relatively simple question to find an answer to. On the matter of the influence of the papers upon public opinion, Bücher held almost a conspiratorial image: 'Everything is thought out in advance (for the reader). In every corner, in every little notice of the paper, the news-reports are mixed in with value judgments, opinions and feelings. In the end this foreign conception weighs down upon one's own powers of judgment as lead.' He went on about the 'suggestivity of printed matter' and about the morality of the press which becomes the 'morality of the masses.' His conceptualization of mass communication was of the cultural-critical variety, and not geared to empirical testing. His idea of public opinion was that of something undifferentiated and irrational, subject to wide and irregular fluctuations [28, p. 53]: 'Public opinion is the judgment of society, strongly saturated with affectual and will components, a mass-psychological reaction which turns affirmatively or negatively against certain events, measures or established facts.' In this conceptualization the question whether certain individuals and groups are more suspectible than others of being influenced by various modes of communication was never raised because public opinion was not thought of as an aggregate of individual opinions.

VI. *Max Weber and the problem of industrial work*

1. *Abbe's experiment*

Before the Verein für Sozialpolitik survey of industrial workers of 1909-1911 is presented, an outline of the range of problems about work which various disciplines were concerned with at this time in Europe will be helpful because the designers of the Verein survey, in particular Max Weber, were familiar with these trends. There was first a great deal of medical work going on, centered on industrial accidents, alcoholism, nourishment and hygiene, and reported in medical journals and all kinds of international conferences and congresses. Then the physiologically oriented psychologists performed laboratory experiments on work from a psychophysics point of view, with a strong emphasis on exact measurement of output, fatigue, muscle movements and the effects of various factors such as temperature, lighting, diet, rest time, etc., upon them. The economists were more directly concerned with the division of labor than with industrial work as such. Nevertheless in Germany they tended to spill over into an area which later became industrial psychology, and which was concerned with fatigue, monotony, and joy of work[1]. Two Verein economists in particular were active in this field: Bücher, who had published *Work and Rhythm* [27] in 1896 and which was based on anthropological data, and Herkner who in 1894 published the *Working Class Question* [61]. Both books eventually ran through several editions. Finally a body of literature was concerned with the relationship between production, length of the working day, and level of wages, and it fed upon some interesting real-life experiments carried out by factory managers with a scientific background. Thus the Belgian chemical engineer Fromont [49] carried out a series of industrial experiment from 1892 to 1905 in a small chemical plant during which he measured the effect on wages and production of a change-

---

[1] 'Joy of work' was the closest equivalent to the present day concept of 'morale'. It carried however the implication that work in itself could be satisfying, whereas morale has more of the connotation of a group property.

over from a two-shift and 12-hour-day to a three-shift and 8-hour day system. The most brilliant of these industrial experiments was that of the German physicist and industrialist Abbe in 1900 whose use of factory records and production registers for making exact measurements in a natural factory setting influenced Max Weber's own study of the productivity of industrial workers.[2]

Abbe was of humble origins. His father had been a worker at the Zeiss optical works, and he had received a scholarship from Zeiss, the founder of the firm. After a brilliant career as a scientist, he joined management and became the head of the firm upon old Zeiss' death. Abbe soon became a pioneer in labor relations through which he hoped a solution to the socio-political problems of the day could be found. In 1901 he became the first industrial manager in Germany to introduce the eight-hour day, but not without first securing the approval of the workers for an experiment whose aim it was to find out whether or not they would earn less by working shorter hours – a prospect that alarmed many of them – and whether or not production would fall and its cost rise – a prospect which alarmed Abbe, for Zeiss had to compete with other firms. The experiment that Abbe conceived [1] was in every respect well designed and successfully carried out. Briefly described, it involved 233 piece-rate workers at Zeiss, all in good health and with more than four years experience at their jobs (to exclude the influence of such factors as on the job learning and physical strength), who for four weeks were kept working nine hours per day, and the following four weeks were shifted to eight hours. A complete record of their earnings was kept, of their production figures, of the number of kilowatt hours of electricity used up by every electric tool they were using (about 650 of them) and whose meter readings were recorded every hour so as to be able to subtract from the total power consumption the amount used by the machines while merely warming up in the morning or idling without being in use.

After the eight weeks were up, Abbe analyzed the results (pp. 246-249) by computing the average earnings of the workers, broken down by age groups and by type of work performed, which indicated clearly that among all the categories of workers without exception earnings had risen slightly in the four weeks during which the eight-hour day

---

[2]   Taylorism was at the time still unknown. Even in the U.S. it became widely known only after the Interstate Commerce Commision hearings in 1910.

had been put into effect.[3] Moreover by an ingenuous analysis of the power-consumption data he was able to show that the cost of production had fallen at the same time because of a more intensive use of the machines. Abbe realized that in order to make exact inferences from his data, he would have to subject it to some sort of statistical analysis, but the figures were such that the differences between means for the eight-hour day and the nine-hour day were significant for all groups of workers. Abbe also felt that some explanation was in order. While the experiment was in progress, he used to walk through the factory and talk to the workers about their attitudes towards the experiment and about their motivation to produce. On the basis of these impressions he wrote (p. 221): 'I consider this question as finally settled, namely it takes no motivation, no good will, no motives of self-interest to bring about an adjustment of the speed of work to the number of hours of work, but that (such adjustment) occurs automatically, even in the case where a certain amount of bad faith might be presumed.' Abbe the physicist would not stop with just such an explanation, but put forward the psycho-physical equation $V=E$, where V, the amount of energy spent, was a function of the amount produced by a worker, the speed at which he worked and the number of hours of work, and E, the energy replacement, was a function of the worker's basic metabolism and the number of hours of rest he enjoyed each day. The parameters of the equation would be different for each individual and for the type of work performed. Abbe thought that an exact scientific treatment of the problem of the optimum number of hours of work from the point of view of maximizing production and minimizing fatigue would involve solving just such a set of equations for every worker in the factory, though he realized that most of the variables and parameters were not susceptible to exact measurement at the time, and the functions of the variables still unknown.

2. Organization of the Verein für Sozialpolitik survey

At the Verein convention in September 1907, Alfred Weber proposed that a survey be made on the influence of factory work in large industrial establishments upon the intellectual and physical qualities of the

---

[3]   When the results of the experiment became known, the workers at Zeiss voted overwhelmingly in favor of the eight-hour day.

workers. Alfred Weber and Bücher thereupon wrote a memorandum upon this question which was discussed at two meetings of the Verein executive committee in the latter half of 1908, a committee of three consisting of Herkner, Schmoller and Alfred Weber was appointed to be directors of the survey, and it then prepared a questionnaire and plan of work for the researchers [152, Vol 133, preface].

In the meanwhile Max Weber had become interested in the survey and took over as its unofficial head. He modified the design and scope of the survey from a descriptive study of the occupational history and life-fate of industrial workers to a more theoretically oriented and explanatory study of the selection and adaptation of workers in large industries [163, p. 1]: 'The present survey aims to establish the following; on the one hand, what influences the large scale industrial establishment exerts upon the individual character, the occupational fate and the style of life of its working force, what physical and psychical qualities it helps develop in it, and how these (qualities) become manifest in the conduct of the daily life of the workers; on the other hand, how the development and the potential future development of large scale industry is limited by those characteristics of the workers which are a result of their ethnic, social and cultural origin, of their traditions and standards of life.'[4] Weber intended the study to be of a scientific nature, the testing of specific hypotheses and exploration of certain theoretical ideas and concepts [163, p. 3]. He mentioned specifically that any recommendations for legislation was to be a byproduct only. He was not aiming at a morphology of factory work consisting of a faithful description of the division of labor, the process of production, and the role of the worker in this process, but at a scientific study of the determinants of production, occupational mobility, and the life cycle of the factory workers [163, p. 4]. On these points the Verein survey was a break with its past social surveys which had a fact-finding character aimed at introducing new legislation or modifying ineffective laws. It was also for the first time that a questionnaire was to be answered directly by the workers. At the same time the researchers were also meant to make use of the factory

---

[4]   Alfred Weber, with whom the idea of the survey had originated, wrote later [145, Vol. 138, p. 148]: 'When I helped to bring the survey into being, my personal interest in it was the clarification of the occupational destiny of industrial workers; later on, of course, more important points of view were incorporated into the survey by other parties.'

office records and to observe the workers directly on the factory floor.

In preparation of the survey Max Weber published a series of articles in the *Archiv* during 1908-9 entitled 'The Psycho-physics of Industrial Work' [164] in which he reviewed the relevant literature and discussed the scientific foundation upon which the survey rested. He also reported some exploratory computations and analyses of workers' production records that he had carried out in the summer of 1908. These articles were some 200 pages in length and show that Weber had absorbed the relevant literature in several fields, in particular psychology, medicine and psychiatry.[5] He also distributed a 60-page monograph entitled 'Methodological Introduction for the Survey of the Verein für Sozialpolitik on the Selection and Adaptation (Occupational Choice and Occupational Fate) of the Workers in Large Industries' [163] which was to serve as an additional guide to a team of younger researchers who were to carry the survey into the field and actually perform the tabulations and analysis. From 1909 to 1911 the survey was carried out, several volumes based on it published [152, Vol. 133-135] and the findings discussed at the 1911 Verein convention [152, Vol. 138].

3. *Weber's conceptualization and aims*

Max Weber spent the summer and part of the fall of 1908 working away at his *Psychophysics of Industrial Work* [164], 'long weeks plunged deeply in the account books and production registers of the weaving mill at Oerlinghäusen'[6] – as Marianne Weber wrote about her husband [158, p. 345] – 'The laborious calculations fare well in his hands, he is gay.'[7] It started with a statement that the recent progresses made in

---

[5] In this connection [164, p. 249] Weber referred to Freud's theories of hysteria and neuropathology as 'increasingly fading'; an interesting instance of one great man's mistaken evaluation of the potentialities of another.

[6] The mill belonged to relatives of Weber who gave him *carte blanche* for his investigations.

[7] Weber's attitude towards the tedious and pedestrian tasks of social research was colored both by a strong ethical commitment to work as such and by their usefulness as an important source of inspiration and of ideas. In his famous address 'Science as a Vocation,' Weber drew on his personal experiences when he told the students [169, p. 135]: 'No sociologist, for instance, should think himself too good, even in his old age, to make tens of thousands of quite trivial computations in his head and perhaps for months at a time. One cannot with impunity try to transfer this task entirely to mechanical assistants if one wishes to figure out something, even though the final result is often small indeed.'

the psychological sciences have not yet been made use of in the socio-economic analysis of work, and the task Weber set himself was to explore precisely how fruit-ful such a collaboration might be. The tone of the monograph was set by the following sentence which expressed the approach from the point of view of psychophysics (p. 63): 'For all the socio-economic problems of modern (especially of large scale industrial) work, the starting point of the investigation should 'in principle' be the physiological and psychological factors of per-formance-ability (in specific tasks). No matter on what the presence of performance-ability in a specific task rests in an individual – whether it be hereditary factors, upbringing, nutrition, or other characteristics of one's life fate that were of determining influence – always his per-formance-ability will become manifest in practice in his psychophysical mechanism.' By psychophysical investigation Weber meant mainly the work of his Heidelberg colleague, the experimental psychologist Kraepelin, which consisted of a search for the factors determining the production curve and its fluctuations obtained by carefully measuring the amount of work through time performed by a subject in the laboratory under various experimental conditions. For some 40 pages Weber reviewed in detail the conceptual apparatus of the Kraepelin experiments: variables such as fatigue, recovery (from fatigue), exercise viewed in terms of muscle movements, speed of work, type of tasks, skill, length of rest periods, monotony and habit, attentiveness con-ditioned by the disturbances of the environment such as noise, etc. Weber even explored the possibility of including social factors not usually considered by the Kraepelin school into the psycho-physical conceptual scheme (pp. 86-87): 'The partly observed and partly assumed de-pendence of the qualifications for a given occupation on influences incurred by the individual at the time of his greatest plasticity, that is in his early youth, one might classify under the loose notion of 'preliminary experience.'' These experiences, including education, religion, city or country upbringing, economic status of the family, jobs during youth such as helping out the parents, and military service 'are rightly considered important determinants of those abilities which are of the utmost importance for the use of a population in industry.'[8]

[8] Note that Weber was here not concerned with the attitudinal and motivational aspect of these socializing influences, but quite specifically with learning ability, physical skills, ability to concentrate, and the like. In part this point of view might be accounted for by some of the experimental results of Kraepelin, which indicated that (pp. 67-68) 'the direct influence of such factors as 'joy of work' and 'morale'

The second section of the study was specifically concerned with transferring this conceptual apparatus from the laboratory into the real life setting of the factory in order to make observations on a mass basis. The main difficulty, as Weber saw it (pp. 118-119), was the introduction of uncontrolled variables, ranging all the way from the life of the worker outside the factory – nourishment, alcohol consumption, sexual life – through the kind of remuneration and type of work, which produce a much more intricate and complicated inducement to work than the simple tasks demanded in the laboratory and the kind of pay inducement which helps sustain a maximum level of performance through the experiment's entire duration.[9] Weber then spent a dozen pages on the problems of measuring worker-output and labor productivity when so much depended on the quality of the fabric, the delays caused by machine breakdown, and other diverse factors.

The next few pages (pp. 132-136) touched upon the methodological core of the investigation and are also the most difficult to understand, partly because Weber was unsure of himself and relief upon philosophical notions, partly because even today the issues are far from being settled. 'In the attempt to analyze causally the fluctuations in production, whether they be expressed in terms of piecerate earnings, or 'exactly' in terms of the figures established through the output-measuring registers, one has to take into account that several categories of components come into play, quite distinct in their manner of 'being given' even though trespassing upon each other's boundaries.' At one end there are factors involving the rational actions of men, 'workers who regulate their output according to plan for material reasons (i.e., gain).... The 'maxims' which such purposeful regulation follows we can 'interpret pragmatically.'' At the other end are factors involving physiological and psychophysical changes which become visible only through their effect, the change in output, and which the workers experience as facilitating or impeding production, without even being aware of the mechanism behind it. Weber cited as example the Zeiss experiment of Abbe where the working day was

---

upon performance-ability, when compared to such a physiological state of being as 'fatigue'... are a lot less important than is generally assumed today.'

[9] Absent from the discussion was the fact that in the laboratory the subject worked and was observed in isolation, whereas on the factory floor workers worked in groups and interacted with each other.

reduced and production was slightly increased just in such an automatic unconscious way, independent of the good will or ill will of the workers. Such factors can be 'explained' by knowing the psychophysical laws derived from experiments. In between these two extremes is the gray zone of attitudes and frames of mind of which the workers are aware, but which they do not consciously experience as being related to a change in output. Such factors can be made psychologically 'understandable' by the researcher by reconstructing them introspectively.

Weber called these distinctions and classification provisional, expressed in a 'not at all scientifically correct language' and concluded that the existence of these three classes of factors 'do not complicate beyond measure a purely psychophysical treatment of industrial work.' Now this three-way classification of causal factors and the three operations of interpretation, explanation and understanding derived from Weber's epistemological thinking and were in agreement with the position he had taken on the issue of the difference between the natural sciences and the cultural sciences. It was potentially confusing from a research point of view which would approach the problem of causal factors from the side of their possible measurement, and the directness or indirectness of their influence upon the effect, the output of the worker. If the existence of motives and attitudes as entities alongside of the physiological factors is recognized, and Weber certainly did recognize them, then the heart of the problem should be their measurement, whether or not they were 'rational,' 'experienced' or 'unconscious.' Of course the *method* of measurement would differ: for example rational motives which the worker is conscious of he might be able to verbalize, whereas the unconscious motives or states of mind might have to be gotten out of him through projective devices. Furthermore the question of the possibility of measurement should again be kept distinct from the related problem of how good a particular measure is. The consequence of all this for the Verein survey and Weber's own computations was not that motivation and attitudes were left out of the discussion, but that they were left to be reconstructed introspectively and made psychologically understandable rather than measured directly in some way and then treated in the analysis formally the same way as 'age,' 'previous occupation' or any of the other variables in the questionnaire or the factory records.

Weber then discussed (pp. 133-136) another methodological problem which he solved in principle quite in the spirit of present day procedure: 'Methodologically important is the specific question whether an exhaustive causal analysis: 1. of a few individual production and earning curves or 2. of the total sum of figures expressed as averages... will yield a better knowledge of the factors of productivity.' He decided for the individual case history approach as a necessary first step because such a step would reveal the direct influence of specific factors upon single individuals' production output clearer than would the pooled results of a large number of them and, equally important, would give the researcher a good feeling just how far the data and figures could be trusted.

In the remaining hundred pages Weber carried out just such an exhaustive analysis of a number of individual production and earning curves in order to determine 'just what chances an attempt might have to trace the differences in worker output back to such sources as inherited characteristics, cultural, social and occupational environment.' The variety of the factors explored ranged from the influence of humidity, the temperature, the time of the day, sex, age, the type of work, the quality of the fabric being worked with, etc. He even followed the fluctuations of output over ten months of one single weaver who had been shifted to a new machine in order to study the influence of experience and the process of learning. Weber had an ability to make a series of numbers tell quite a story, and his manipulation of the original data were ingenious and his conclusions were carefully qualified. For example (pp. 147-152) he discovered a pattern in the weekly output curve that consisted of a slow start on Mondays, followed by a rise to maximum output on Wednesdays, than a slackening on Thursday back almost to the Tuesday level followed by a slower rise till Saturday. But since this pattern was derived from the aggregate data of several weavers over several weeks, he examined each work week of each weaver separately to determine the day of the week when maximum performance occurred, then computed the percent of maximum performances that occurred on each day. Again Monday showed the lowest percent, Wednesday the highest. But Weber was still not satisfied: he examined each separate output curve again, and for each day counted the number of times production had either increased or decreased with respect of the preceding day, then compared the days of the week on this measure. These results and an earlier examination of the frequency of accidents by days of the week led him to the *tentative* hypothesis that for weaving at least a pattern of output did exist, and might be explained in terms of fatigue and recovery, except for the low Monday output which reflected the influence of alcohol consumption on Sundays. Even so Weber wrote that there might exist several such typical patterns, depending upon other characteristics of the workers such as their family origin or other circumstances such as the type of work performed.

Rather than outline all the other factors that Weber examined, we shall discuss in detail how he approached the question of voluntary restriction of output for it is a key to an understanding of why he conceptualized industrial work from the point of view of psychophysics.[10] The Hawthorne experiments conducted by Elton Mayo and his associates in the thirties, which pioneered the development of industrial sociology, also started out with the idea that the output of the workers was mainly a function of 'psychophysical' variables such as lighting, humidity, temperature, etc., and that by improving the physical environment the workers would raise their output. After several years of experimentation and paradoxical findings, the Hawthorne researchers discovered that the workers' motivation and behavior had to be understood in the context of the groups in which they were working and participating. The level of output of the workers could only be explained with reference to the norms and values which the work group had created and maintained. Was Max Weber and the Verein für Sozialpolitik researchers unaware that individuals at work interact and that these interactions in turn have a decisive influence upon the workers' attitudes, motivation, and output?

Weber identified two types of restriction of output (pp. 155-157): one was conscious and purposeful, the other depended on one's mood or frame of mind. These two types were consistent with his earlier classification of factors influencing production. The first type was purposeful, calculated action, the second type was traditional in orientation and 'economically irrational,' and corresponded to the dispositions and attitudes classified earlier in category three. The purposeful restriction of output Weber saw as a form of socio-political

---

[10]   The reason Weber himself gave (p. 63) was that the study was meant to explore how far the conceptual apparatus and exact methods of the experimental psychological sciences might be applicable to the investigation of industrial work in its factory setting. The matter is however more complicated because it does not explain why Weber held the psychophysical frame of reference as adequate or sufficiently flexible for his own purpose.

protest against the entrepreneur, and he analyzed (pp. 158, 228-230) in detail the performance figures of a worker who was single-handedly doing just that over several months. Elsewhere he pointed out that the high performers among the workers 'are compelled to restrict their output directly or indirectly through the solidarity of their fellow workers' because of the danger that it might lead to an up-grading of the work norms. But such purposeful behavior was con-ceptualized as an exceptional and temporary phenomenon, and not as a usual consequence of work in groups. As an example of the second kind of behavior, of traditional values which became manifest in performance, he cited (pp. 161-162) the output figures of female workers from a pietist background (which in this case was not a restriction of output but a production beyond the norm): 'The shun-ning of dance halls and other such pleasures condemned by 'Pietism,' the consequences of the 'asceticism of Protestantism' and of the inner orientation towards the 'God-willed' worldly occupation sus-tained through it, express themselves clearly in such observations.... One will have to examine carefully how far such manifestations have still today a general significance – That they belong, as residues of the past, into the wider currents which I have attempted to analyze elsewhere, and that they are still to some extent characteristic of the same forces which were operative in the early epoch of capitalism, seems credible to me.'[11]

Neither of these two types of behavior were seen by Weber as resulting form 'communal' social relationships (*Vergemeinschaftung*). Indeed Weber did not think that under the prevailing bureaucratic

[11] Conversely the following reference to the psychophysics studies may be found in *The Protestant Ethic and the Spirit of Capitalism* [161, p. 62:] 'One often hears, and statistical investigation confirms it, that by far the best chances of economic education are found among this group (of Pietist girls).' [See also footnote 24 in Chapter I]. There is other evidence to demonstrate that Weber did not segregate his cultural-historical studies from contemporary-empirical investigations. In 'The Social-Psychology of World Religions' one reads the following [167, p. 275]: 'The rational need for a theodicy of suffering and of dying has had extremely strong effects.... Even as late as 1906, a mere minority among a rather considerable number of proletarians gave as reasons for their disbelief in Christianity conclusions derived from modern theories of natural science. The majority, however, referred to the 'injustice' of the order of this world – to be sure, essentially because they be-lieved in a revolutionary compensation in this world.' This statement was based on Weber's examination of the Levenstein questionnaire answers, specifically questions 22, 23, and 24.

organization of industry, regardless of whether it was capitalist or socialist, the workers were masters of their destiny even to a small degree. This view was made explicit in the last two pages of his methodological introduction where the modern factory was described in the following terms: 'Its hierarchic authority structure, its discipline, its chaining of the men to the machines, its spatial aggregation and yet isolation of the workers (in comparison with the spinning rooms of the past), its formidable accounting system that reaches down to the simplest hand movement of the worker...' In this impersonal system of total control, the principle of selection according to least cost and highest output prevailed and completely determined the occupational destiny of the worker.[12] If the worker was no more than a cogwheel in a piece of big machinery, then his contribution to the production process had to be analyzed in mechanical terms. It was this conception that led Weber to approach the problem of factory work from the point of view of psychophysics to the relative neglect of the social organization of the workers in the factory and the socialpsychological aspects of their relationship to each other and to work.

That in spite of this approach Weber's insights into the internal stratification of the workers, their status-sequence and socializing processes make for fascinating reading may be seen from one of many questions raised [163, p. 53]: 'To what extent is the distribution of workers by their place of origin among the various types of jobs not only a result of their abilities to perform that particular type of job, but a result of the reasons of their social evaluation of the particular jobs? (One example: the seamstresses in textile factories evaluate their own type of work higher than the higher paid work of the female weavers, because it is cleaner and resembles domestic house work, and as a result one observes a more marked recruitment into seamstress-jobs on the part of city-raised women)'. Weber by no means wanted the researchers to neglect (pp. 53 ff.) the 'subjective attitudes' of the workers to their work, what motives other than pecuniary ones

---

[12] The parallelism between Weber's conception of industrial organization and the Darwinian world of stuggle for survival is made further evident in the double title of the survey. Originally it was called the survey of 'occupational choice and occupational destiny' of the workers in large industries. When Max Weber took over its direction, he added to the title the phrase 'selection and adaptation' of the workers.

operated in the various groups, what their attitude towards rest periods were, towards monotony, towards the prestige attached to the various occupations: 'Do the differences in occupation, the degree of acquired skills, the position inside the factory, lead to social intercourse and social bonds quite apart from associations based upon sheer economic interests? And if yes, where does the boundary lie, and according to what criteria do the workers draw the line in social intercourse?' But these 'subjective attitudes' of the workers were not made part of Verein questionnaire despite their importance, because they belong into the shadow-area of human actions, in between the conscious, purposeful actions and the physiological motorreactions (pp. 53-54): 'Such and similar questions, as they are contained in the 'research outline' will not be answered easily by the workers, often without any certainty at all. The circumstances that the workers are unable to do so... in itself appears as characteristic of their total state of mind and is also of importance for the survey. For just that which appears as so *self-evident* to a segment of the population and, because of it, is not openly expressed by them, and second, that which remains *unconscious* for it, because it rests on countless suggestions of their specific environment, just these matters are the most important components of their inner attitude toward their condition in life.' All such questions were to be observed by establishing a personal contact between the researcher and the workers. The ambivalent position that Weber took towards these 'subjective' factors was all the more surprising as he was thoroughly familiar with Levenstein's questionnaire and its results, and as was mentioned above, persuaded Levenstein to analyze attitude questions exactly in the same way as he suggested production-curves be analyzed, namely by cross-tabulating them by age, earning, type of work and other available background variables.

Before the questionnaire and the outcome of the Verein survey are taken up, one remaining issue has to be dealt with. This issue, the extent to which the processes of biological inheritance are an ultimate source upon which many social processes rest, also ran through much of Weber's later work without ever receiving an answer that satisfied him. In the 1920 Introduction that Weber wrote to the sociology of world religions [161], the last paragraph read as follows (pp. 30-31): 'Finally, we may make a reference to the anthropological side of the problem. When we find again and again that, even in departments of life apparently mutually independent, certain types of rationalization have developed in the Occident, and only there, it would be natural to suspect that the most important reasons lay in differences of heredity. The author admits that he is inclined to think that importance of biological heredity very great. But in spite of the notable achievement of anthropological research, I see up to the present no way of exactly or even approximately measuring either the extent or, above all, the form of its influence on the development investigated here. It must be one of the tasks of sociological and historical investigation first to analyze all the influences and causal relationships which can satis-factorily be explained in terms of reactions to environmental con-ditions. Only then, and when comparative racial neurology and psychology shall have progressed beyond their present and in many ways promising beginnings, can we hope for even the probability of a satisfactory answer to the problem.'[13] The reason for the extensive quote is that it illustrates many aspects of Weber's work that are not usually emphasized: he was concerned with the problem of inheritance, and saw it in terms of a problem of *measurement*; furthermore he had actually *tried* to measure its extent empirically (without success – this explains the extremely pessimistic tone of his statement); and lastly, even at such an unlikely place as here, in the analysis and history of rationalism, he tried to link up his empirical investigation with his cultural and historical studies.

In the study on industrial work Weber estimated [164, pp. 242-255] that hereditary factors were important in the extent of development of the nervous and physical constitution of the workers, which in turn were determining factors of performance-ability, yet he clearly saw that many environmental factors, such as being brought up in the city, receiving an education, might produce exactly the same results. Furthermore the socializing influences during childhood and youth might either reinforce or dampen the effect of hereditary forces. He also noted that the biologists themselves were not agreed as to precisely what might be inherited, and he intended to stay clear of all their con-troversies. The empirical demonstration of the presence of hereditary factors could only be valid if all the environmental factors were held

---

[13] Another reference to inheritance problems may be found in the 1913 article 'Über einige Kategorien der Verstehenden Soziologie' [168, p. 101], where Weber speculated that such factors as 'the striving for specific forms of social power'and 'the ability for rational orientation to action' might be in part due to hereditary factors.

constant, and differences in production output still persisted that is
(p. 253): 'if a certain group in the population had gone through a
specific occupational experience in one generation, and then in the
next generation demonstrated a differential qualification of magnitude
x for that occupation.' Heredity would then become a residual
explanation by default. In appraising Weber's concern for hereditary
influences it must not be forgotten that at the turn of the century the
question of inherited characteristics was in general vastly overestimated
in importance, and that scientific studies of criminality, insanity,
suicide, and even of the moral and spiritual condition of the working
class could not bypass this point of view.

4. The questionnaire and the outcome of the survey

The questionnaire centered on several of the topics discussed above.
Questions 11, 13, 18-22 were intended to contribute primarily to the
psychophysical analysis of the workers' earning and output records.
Weber hoped that such variables as the distance and manner of
transportation to the factory, the kinds of leisure time activities and
the manner of nourishment would contribute to their analysis.
Questions 5-7 and 26 on the occupation and military fitness of four
generations of a family were intended to test hypotheses about inheritance. Many of the other questions dealt with the detailed occupational history and life-fate of the worker, from the choice of an
occupation and his apprenticeship (questions 9, 10) to his means of
survival in old age (questions 10, 27) and the style of life of his family
(questions 22-26).[14] The two departures from the otherwise matter-
of-fact nature of the questionnaire were question 10 on the reason for
choice of occupation and question 27 on life-goals. The evidence
points to the fact that the Verein committee was well aware of
their rather exploratory nature.[15] The vast question on life-goals
was the only direct attempt to get at aspirations and attitudes
directly.

[14]   These issues were Alfred Weber's stake in the Verein study.
[15]   Weber's own attitude was reflected in the remarks he made at the 1911 Verein
meetings [152, Vol. 138, p. 192] that the real reasons for occupational choice may
have nothing to do with the actual reasons that people will give, still 'one receives
quite valuable answers to even stupid questions.'

Verein Questionnaire

1. Name....Position....with company...
2. Year of birth...Place of birth...Country....
3. Sex and Family Status: M or F, married, single, separated, widowed....
4. Religion....
5. Occupation and Place of Birth, of father....,of mother....
6. Occupation of grandfathers....
7. Military service: has served, not yet served, fitness, has your father been in the service?....
8. Education...where?....
9. Apprenticeship: what kind and where? how long? paid for.... How much?... or did you get wages?... from what date on?....
10. For what reason have you taken up this occupation?....
11. What kind of work do you perform in your present position?...
12. Do you possess other occupational skills than the ones you are presently making use of?... which ones?
13. Is your work especially strenuous?... How?...
14. At what age do people in your work-situation find it ño longer easy to get a job?....
15. Have you been in other jobs in the past? Where... for how long... In what job...
16. Reasons for changing jobs....
17. Are you on time- or piece-rate?.... Approximate weekly earnings? ...Which do you prefer, time- or piece-rates?...
18. Duration of work day: from... o'clock to... o'clock. Rest periods.... Overtime... at what time do you take your main meal?....
19. After how many hours of work do you generally start getting tired?....
20. What are your recuperating activities?....
21. What is your favorite activity outside of your occupation?....
22. Living quarters: Own house...apartment... supplied by employer... only a bed... distance of home to work...km; do you ride to work...; do you own a plot of land or garden...; cultivate it yourself....
23. Do you rents bed?... do you have boarders?... how many?....
24. Do you have a second source of income?.... What is it?....
25. When did you get married?... Does your wife earn money?.... How?...
26. Number of children?.... Of these there are still alive.... male.... female.... List of living children.
    Rank First name Age Occupation Apprenticeship Military Status
    Why these occupations in particular?....
    Approximate earnings of the children....
27. Which goal in life do you hope to reach?....
    Which goal did you set yourself earlier?....
    How do you expect to make a living during old age?....

Addenda: detailed occupational history of worker, with location, type of work, length of time, pay, reasons for leaving.

In the research-outline [145, Vol. 133, preface] which accompanied the questionnaire, the Verein researchers were urged to establish by direct observation and conversation with the workers a number of other matters including 'alleged and real motives of the workers for or against changes in geographical location, factory, and occupation (within a factory),' whereas the actual amount of such mobility was to be established from the occupational history data and the factory records. Similarly the internal stratification of the factory workers due to the division of labor and the social composition of the upwardly mobile work-force were included among the points to be established, but no specific procedure was suggested to the researchers on how to go about it. The researchers were told that the 'characteristics of a closed social group along occupational lines' was consciousness of belonging together, intermarriage, social intercourse, similarity of styles of life, and so on, but it was not suggested that quality or manner of clothing be observed as visible signs of status differences (as in fact the researchers occasionally reported later). The whole area of the social organization of the factory floor, of the preference of the different groups of workers for different types of occupations, of their attitude towards advancement and their satisfaction with the pay and the work, of their relationships with fellow workers, this whole area of factory life was not the focus of the analysis and received only secondary attention in the design of the study.

From 1909 to 1911 a dozen eager researchers carried the study to its rather unhappy conclusion. The main reason for this was the almost total refusal on the part of the workers to answer the questionnaire. A Dr. Heiss who was supposed to survey a large Berlin factory got back less than 200 out of 3,500 questionnaires handed out, another researcher 283 out of 2,500, still another 173 out of 1,800. Another was so discouraged after getting back only 100 out of 4,000 questionnaires that he simply quit [152, Vol. 138, p. 121]. It would seem that even where the unions could be persuaded at least not to condemn the survey, the workers were 'mistrustful.' Some researchers did achieve partial results. An engineer, Dr. Bienkowski, did establish production-output curves of a limited number of workers by making use of the available factory records as Weber had done. Rosa Kempf, working through Brentano's seminar, did carry out an interesting field study of 'the life of young factory girls in Munich,' during which she visited quite a few of the girls' homes, described their family and factory life in detail (for example the menus of meals were given in full for several families, and the inventory of clothes of some of the factory girls), but her study departed completely from the design of the Verein survey. Only Marie Bernays, who was Weber's *protégée*, did succeed in administering the questionnaire to most of the workforce in a factory.

Marie Bernays got herself hired incognito as a factory worker in a textile-mill where she first spent four months working, observing and making friends before she administered the questionnaire and immersed herself into the factory's records. Her report [10] contained some excellent observations and ingenious methods of analysis, but these were unfortunately often hampered by the small size of her population. For example (p. 244) she crosstabulated 'present occupation' by 'goals for the future' in youth (expressed as an occupation), and then introduced 'father's occupation' into the relationship to check on this important source of occupational plans, but over half of her table cells became empty. Bernays managed to get complete data from the factory office records on three years, 1891, 1900, and 1908, for a trend study of the shifting composition of the workers. In one of these tables (p. 58) the entries in the table crossclassifying some 15 occupational groups with age categories are the percent of workers who have stayed on in the factory from beginning to end of the year.[16] Then she ranked the various occupational groups by the degree of their 'stability' and 'mobility' as expressed in these figures, and noted: 'That the degree of stability is a function of the higher social standing of a group is made plausible when we compare the degree of stability of the individual groups, and find that the 'aristocracy' of the factory – the mechanics – are very stable, but that its 'proletariat' – the dye-mixers – are very mobile.' In an adjoining footnote she wrote further: 'Which qualities actually make up this 'higher social standing' that one feels immediately in personal contact with people is hard to say. Perhaps a more careful education, a more purposeful conduct of one's life, a greater proximity to culture, if one might describe it briefly.' Elsewhere (p. 141) Bernays established that the more skilled workers were more likely to change from one factory or town to another, without changing their occupation, whereas for the unskilled workers the opposite was relatively more likely. In her attempt to find out how far the monotony of work

[16] She called these percentages *Restprozente*. Today they are known as transition probabilities.

was to be accountable for job turnover she was again led by her own observations outside of Weber's design (p. 168): 'When this fear of lower pay was dispelled, then the remaining dislike of the workers against a change of jobs originated of a strong attachment to their accustomed place at work from which they separated only grudgingly. ...'One would like to know definitely where one belongs to' is what the female workers implied as they expressed the desire to have a little realm for themselves, even if it was only a few feet long and if its boundaries consisted of empty boxes.' Later in a chapter entitled 'Werkstatt-Gemeinschaft' she described how the factory was divided into a multitude of separate, solidary groups (p. 183): 'The different rooms in the factory have a definite character, which is visible in the appearance and nature of the people in them, even in their manner of dress....' and she suggested that 'this separation of great masses of workers in a factory into individual small groups plays a role for the psyche of the worker that should not be underestimated: I would suggest that it saves him from sinking into the mass, from becoming a mere number, inasmuch as there exists a small circle to which he can belong and in which he can achieve some recognition.'

But Marie Bernays did not consider these observations the high point of her efforts. The second part of her study consisted of an analysis of production curves and figures for various occupations which followed quite faithfully Weber's own outline in his psychophysics monograph, and it is these results that she reported at the Verein meetings of 1911 where the survey was discussed. She examined the relationship of age, marital status, occupation of father, size of locality of birth, length of the working day, type of home, with output. The results of the analysis were inconclusive. Age alone showed a clear relationship in all occupations, both among males and females, with a drop in output starting around 35 years of age. The strong effect of age would have required that it be partialled out in all the other tables, but the limited number of cases in each occupation made this impracticable. Furthermore Bernays was able to confirm the fluctuations of output by the day of the week and the hour of the day that Weber had found in his data, but this was a low yield if one remembers that Weber had hoped to detect the influence of hereditary factors upon productivity by comparing the output of weavers whose parents and grandparents had already been textile workers with those whose ancestors had been peasants.

The Verein für Sozialpolitik meetings of 1911 [152, Vol. 138] were astonishing for the lack of critical appraisal about what had actually been established through the survey. Heinrich Herkner, who in his student days in Brentano's seminar had conducted a small survey among Alsatian factory workers [60] and since then had become recognized as an expert on the psychology of workers [61], was the main speaker. He quoted the figures on the non-returned questionnaires, deplored them, and then proceeded to sketch a picture of factory work and the state of the working class as though it were based on a firm body of findings. Alfred Weber recommended on the basis of a few productivity curves that a law on compulsory saving be passed, withholding from the worker part of his pay to be paid back to him later in life when his income was on the decline. In a subsequent article [157] in which he expanded upon this theme, it is interesting to note that wherever he mentioned the psychological aspects of working class life and work, his source was Levenstein's survey and the worker biographies, not the Verein studies. Only the statistician Bortkiewitz mentioned the danger of making inferences from a small and unrepresentative number of cases. He suggested improvements in the questionnaire based upon his experience with official and census surveys. He pointed out that for women, the question on the choice of an occupation should be split into two parts. First, why are you working at all, and second, why in this particular factory, in this occupation. Bortkiewitz also pointed out a number of crude mistakes that had been made in the computations, especially that of percentages based on the wrong base number, and recommended a higher level of statistical know-how for social researchers as well as supervision of their work by competent statisticians. Towards the end of the discussion Max Weber at last spoke up rather reluctantly. He realized that the enthusiasm of most of the speeches was unjustified and sought first of all to bring home to the audience the limited result of the survey [152, Vol. 138, pp. 190-191]: 'There has been talk... of the great 'findings' of these surveys, of magnificent studies that have been made.... No definite results have so far been accomplished, nothing more than a few numbers to support a few hypotheses, to change some others, to correct the manner of questioning and – this is the most important point by far – to prove that the data which was used here... will in time, and it will be a rather long period of time, yield valuable and definitive results with high probability.' He acknowledged and answered most of Bortkiewitz's criticism whose comments Weber said were most to the point and most helpful. In the strongest terms Weber sought nonetheless to encourage among the younger generation a scientific, selfless devotion to empirical and computational work in their dissertations even if definitive results would not be accomplished, but only stepping stones for future scientific work.

5. *Reception of the Verein survey and of Levenstein's attitude survey*

Since both the Verein survey and Levenstein's attitude survey were published within a few months of each other and dealt to some extent with a similar problem area, it is instructive to compare their reception and pursue their fate in the years that followed. Herkner [62] gave Levenstein an unfavorable and rather snobbish bookreview, classifying him into the 'pretentious stratum' of workers. Herkner felt that many of the questions were 'suggestive' and that the quantitative analysis of the answers was not valuable. He preferred the earlier Levenstein publications of workers' poems, letters and essays, and even went as far as to say that the Verein survey had shed more light on workers' morale and attitude towards work than Levenstein. Marie Bernays [12], who reviewed Levenstein for the *Archiv*, also wrote an unfavorable review in which she failed to show appreciation for a quantitative treatment of attitudes. She did, however, admit reluctantly that 'it is for the first time that a survey of mass psychology reveals such personal experiences....' This injustice was corrected a year later when the young social psychologist and friend of Max Weber, Willy Hellpach, wrote an additional 10-page bookreview in the *Archiv*, prefaced by an editorial note that Bernays had not paid enough attention to the socialpsychological side of it. Hellpach [57] saw in the answers of the workers to the questions on monotony, fatigue and thoughts during work a valuable contribution to an understanding of the motivation to work. He also recognized the forest question (#25) as a projection device for wish fulfillment.[17] Despite his generally

[17] Examples of answers received by Levenstein to this question were [88, p. 370]: 'When I lie thus down in the forest and observe the vehicles passing by on the road and see their splendor and think about myself, I am filled with despair'; and (p. 363): 'When I go into the forest I think of the life of primitive man, of the freshness of the air in those days when no factory chimneys had yet polluted it.'

favorable appraisal Hellpach remained ambivalent about the future use of attitude surveys: 'Answers to surveys can never become the starting point for exact calculations.' After the war he became more convinced of the importance of Levenstein's accomplishments [58, pp. 40-41]: 'A true attempt to penetrate into the world of real attitudes and wishes of the German factory worker beyond the usual journalistic cliches is available: it is Adolph Levenstein's monumental survey, monumental in its conception and in its analysis of the data despite some serious errors and painful gaps in the procedure. This attempt has remained the only one of its kind; everything that we know about the inner life of factory workers originates from it.' Hugo Münsterberg, the father of industrial psychology, was also familiar with the Levenstein survey, but failed to recognize the potentialities of attitude surveys. In the English-language edition of *Psychology and Industrial Efficiency* [102] he quoted from Levenstein on such matters as fatigue, pleasure at work, thoughts during work and recreation, but wrote (p. 238): 'Yet, all taken together, even such a careful investigation on a psycho-statistical basis stongly suggests that a few careful experimental investigations could lead further than such a heaping up of material gathered from men who are untrained in self-observation and above all who arc accessible to any kind of suggestion and preconceived idea.' In a more scholarly German book in 1914 Münsterberg devoted more space to Levenstein without changing his basic assessment [103, pp. 405-409]. He used the material to illustrate how much more complicated the mind was than was generally assumed, and to disprove the notion that repetitive work necessarily led to monotony. It is important to note that Münsterberg never discussed those aspects of the survey concerned with the hopes, wishes, aspirations, and expectations of the workers, but rather the fatigue and monotony data, and seemed to have been under the impression that Levenstein had merely tried out a substitute method for laboratory experiments. Nor did Münsterberg or others who here and there refer to Levenstein's findings ever look beyond the marginals of a given question and check whether different groups of workers (by age, income, occupation and location) had given a different set of answers and why this might be so. Had Münsterberg been more impressed, he might have called Levenstein's work to the attention of American social science when he transferred to Harvard as professor of psychology.[18]

[18] The Levenstein questionnaire exerted, however, an indirect influence upon a

On the other hand the psychological literature on factory work abounded with references to Weber's psychophysics paper and Bernays' results. Whereas before the war most of the work in this area was carried out in Belgium, France and the U.S., a flood of German investigations and books on productivity, psychophysics, psychotechnics, the eight-hour day, etc., were published in the twenties, and most of them mentioned the productivity-curves that Weber and Bernays had established as a significant finding. Münsterberg in particular was much more impressed with them than with Levenstein. On Weber he wrote [102, p. 149]: 'These experiences... concerning the influences of training, the mechanization of repetition and the automatization of movement have been thoroughly discussed by a brilliant political economist as an explanation of certain industrial facts, but they have not yet practically influenced life in the factory.' Münsterberg was thus much more convinced than Weber himself about the validity of the findings. Willy Hellpach was on the main critical of the Verein survey results and even its design [58, p. 41]: 'I have repeatedly called the attention of the deceased Max Weber to the fact that the analysis could be psychologically fruitful only if we already possessed the psychological key to the storehouse of its statistical materials.' Yet Hellpach's overall conceptualization of factory work remained basically very much like Weber's own [58, p. 31]: 'In the factory the work-community is on final analysis restricted to a spatial proximity of many workers without any essential or human interconnection.' He contrasted this atomization with the talk and laughter of earlier spinning rooms, the exact same comparison that Weber had made in the same context. However Hellpach did have a keen insight into the psychological aspects of factory work [58, pp. 37-39]. He drew a masterful comparison between administrative work and factorywork. Administrative tasks are just as boring, atomized and petty as industrial work, but they are made psychologically more attractive by social recognition of white collar work, visible in such things as a salary rather than wages, in the possibility of advancement and security in retirement. In

line of development which has come to be one of the main areas of empirical research and theory in social psychology. In the 1930s the Horkheimer and Fromm group which conducted extensive studies on authority and the family in Germany and Europe mentioned [68, p. 232] Levenstein among the predecessors of their questionnaire survey methodology. Later this same group was to conduct the studies on the authoritarian personality in the U.S.

factory work however 'a feeling of worth and self respect is not created by the rewards of one's life long activities, but by knowig how indispensable the work is for society, despite its monotony and harshness.'

6. *A note on the non-ideal type bureaucracy*

Weber's description of bureaucracy in *Wirtschaft und Gesellschaft* has become widely known among sociologists. It is the starting point of of scholarly publications and textbooks on the theory of organizations. It is also customary to point out that Weber's ideal type is an incomplete description of bureacratic structure and that it has to be combined with an account of the informal organization of bureaucracy. It is generally not known that in some of his speeches and little known writings, Weber himself described certain features of bureaucracy which were either not mentioned or in contradiction with his ideal type formulation. It is true however that he did not elaborate on these ideas in systematic fashion.

At the convention of the Verein für Sozialpolitik in 1909, the debate centered on whether municipal ownership of public utilities and transportation was preferable to private ownership from the point of view of social policy. Weber pointed out [152, Vol. 132, pp. 282-287] that the consequence of substituting state employees for private managers would not necessarily benefit the workers because the civil servants would soon adopt the same attitude toward the workers and the same style of labor relations as the private entrepreneurs: 'Civil servants experience the same frustrations and (go through) the same petty wars with the workers as the private entrepreneur....' He noted that conditions of work and labor relations were extremely poor in the mines owned by the state and said: 'If I were put into such a position (of superior), I could not prevent feeling irritated over the eternal resistance to my so carefully worked out and orderly plans which I would experience in daily friction with the workers and their unions, (and I could not prevent) the desire to send these people to the devil, because as a bureaucrat I would be convinced... that I knew better than these 'nitwits' what is best for themselves.' This statement by Weber stands in sharp contrast to the ideal type bureaucrat who performs his official duties *sine ira ac studio*, and who eliminates all purely personal and emotional elements from his activities. In a similar vein during these debates Alfred Weber said that (pp. 242-3) 'Bureaucracy creates bonds of loyalty of which there is no mention in the formal structure (*Verfassung*), and which render it illusory...', and further, '...it is a fundamental error (to think) that the bureaucracy ...nowhere rests on a social base.' The context makes it clear that Alfred Weber meant that the bureaucracy, far from being neutral, was vulnerable to political pressures and was representative of the interests of the ruling groups and of those strata from which the civil service was largely recruited. These speeches by the Weber brothers were interpreted by the newspapers as an attack on the integrity of the German bureaucracy, and as indicative of the radical and un-orthodox views held by some members of the Verein für Sozialpolitik.

Another source of Weber's ideas on how bureaucracy operates is contained in the unfinished report of his experiences as a volunteer in military hospitals during the first year of World War I. His wife fortunately included the report in her biography [158, pp. 545-60]. At the outbreak of the war Weber was 50 and not physically fit to become an active soldier. Nevertheless he volunteered his services and was made the chief disciplinary officer of the military field hospitals in the Heidelberg district. During the first month of his tenure the hospitals actually had to be built up from scratch. The staff of volunteers, many of them university professors, had to fit out the hospitals with the thousand necessities of life, from hospital beds to bandages and kitchen utensils. At this time the volunteers exercised *de facto* authority over the conduct of operations because the regular medical and administrative staff was slow in reporting to their posts amidst the general confusion of the first few weeks of the war. In time however the improvised volunteer administration was replaced by the professionals. Indeed Weber called his report a case study of the 'transition from a purely dilettante and voluntary administration to an orderly and bureaucratic one.'

Weber observed that during the period of gradual transition friction between the two groups was avoided because the volunteers who stayed with the job took over certain functions which were not specified in the formal structure, but which nevertheless made a significant difference in the overall performance of the hospitals. At first the volunteers assumed charge of the reception and distribution of presents and donations; later they also organized the Christmas celebrations, gave formal instruction to the soldiers in foreing languages, accounting, shorthand, and even delivered a series of lectures on history and economics; they provided cigars, games, room decorations, books, clothes, conversation, and other items geared to individual needs. In short the volunteers took charge of many of the recreational and other non-medical needs of the soldiers during their long period of convalescence. Weber thought that these needs could not be provided for by the hospital staff because of the different nature of their responsibilities. Thus the activities of the volunteers were an essential service for the main problem of the hospitals was maintaining discipline and morale among the convalescing soldiers: 'The practical significance (of the volunteer organization) became evident in the fact that the number of men put under arrest was clearly related to the lack of such a volunteer organization (*Liebesgabenverwaltung*), and that it was the highest where it did not exist and the men were left to face the solitude and the inaction of the hospitals by themselves.' Weber thus directly linked the incidence of deviant behavior with the lack of an effective 'informal' organization of the hospitals.

Finally it seems also relevant to report Weber's observations about the effectiveness of the volunteer nurses in contrast to the professional nurses, since in the ideal type formulation of bureaucracy he usually emphasized the superiority of the professionally trained expert. Weber distinguished between two types of volunteer nurses. One was the typical German 'junge Mädchen', filled with enthusiasm and sentimentality, who was not well suited for providing nursing care because she mothered the patients and often got herself personally involved with them. On the other hand the second type of volunteer nurse, who was in general well educated and who came from a good social background, maintained high morale and effective discipline, and was more effective in handling the patients than the average professional nurse 'because of a more varied and individual approach to the sick, taking care not only of their hygienic and physical, but also of their human and intellectual needs, without a loss of the appropriate distance.'

VII. *Conclusion*

The empirical studies assembled and described in this dissertation show that a considerable amount of social research was done in Germany before World War I. At the same time it was lacking in continuity and did not become institutionalized either in the universities or in organizations such as the Verein für Sozialpolitik. This fact demands an explanation. One must dig deeper than some ready made statements about the grip of historicism upon the German mind and the idealistic legacy in philosphy that prevented the rise of positivism in social science and favored an intuitive and phenomenological approach. The truth is that Germany's intellectual heritage did not prevent the emergence of psychology as science firmly grounded on empirical data and the experimental method, that the political economists were committed to the use of contemporary statistical data and the inductive method, and that historical positivism and research had displaced the philosophy of history.

The one pervasive characteristic of German social research in the period 1848-1914 was its concern with working class people and their problems. It was essentially motivated by the need for action and reform. Already in 1871 Gustav Schönberg said on the occasion of his appointment as a professor [126]: 'We lack at the present time the first precondition for truly great reform: we in Germany are ignorant of the true condition of the working classes and the causes of their ills.' He therefore called for the creation of worker-agencies, run by the government, whose duty it would be to survey periodically the lower classes. Such agencies never came into being, yet a number of religious organizations and associations supporting social reform met this need to some extent by conducting surveys on their own. It should not be surprising, however, that these men who were filled with enthusiasm but lacking in technical skills would soon discover that they had vastly underestimated the tasks of collecting and analyzing survey data. The rewards in terms of usable knowledge were rather slim when compared to the time and effort invested. Most of these organizations conducted but one single survey, and none of them ever established a permanent research unit. Social research did come into being under these circumstances, but it was tied too closely to the energies and fortunes of single individuals to become established beyond them. The small impact which the work of non-academic innovators like Rade, Hofmann, Göhre and Levenstein exercised upon the academic community was probably due as much to its inability to assess properly the nature of these innovations as to the professionals' traditional exclusion of trespassers upon their domain, a characteristic not alone peculiar to the academic community of pre-1914 Germany.

If one turns to the universities a number of factors would at first sight appear to favor the emergence and continuity of an empirical tradition. The academic world is assured of continuity quite apart from the success and failure of particular studies. Its members possess the basic professional skills. The incentive to advance knowledge is ordinarily present and rewarded. As an additional factor in the Germany of the pre-war period, most political economists were extremely interested in matters concerning the economic well-being and the political activities of the lower classes, and they did possess the necessary descriptive statistical skills. Most of them also belonged to the Verein für Sozialpolitik which was ready to sponsor empirical studies and would assure their publication.

Turning to the negative side of the balance, there were powerful factors inhibiting the growth of social research. Sociology was not recognized as an academic discipline. Social scientist meant actually political economist, and at any one time in the 1890s and after, there were no more than sixty of them in all the German universities combined, from lowest instructor to highest professor. Thus there was the question of numbers: these men taught economics, economic history, statistics, administrative history and even political science. Only a fraction of them might realistically be expected to take an active interest in social research, which was yet undefined and marginal to their discipline. Another characteristic which marks the emergence of a new area of knowledge in the academic world is the lack of agreement about what it should consist of and where its boundaries lie. Considerable energy is wasted in polemics that attempt to define these matters. No matter how necessary such debates are for legitimizing a break with past tradition, the danger is that in the intellectual atmosphere of the universities they remain at a high level of abstraction. Certainly the numerous polemics about moral statistics fit into this category, and later on the Mayr-Tönnies feud about statistics and sociography. Then the prestige of the historical and philosophical tradition was still so strong that the political economy departments drew mostly law students bent on a civil service career, and not the best 'arts and science' students. Moreover the manner of turning out doctoral candidates was not geared to the type of persistent and collective effort which is the mark of most good social research. The custom was to attend several universities in quick succession and then to polish off a 50-70-page thesis in one of the political economy seminars.

Still there was the Verein für Sozialpolitik which did carry out some social surveys over a span of 40 years. Although it had a permanent machinery for initiating team research (the executive committee, which would review, approve and financially aid a project), it had no permanent staff to perform the work. The principal investigator had the task of enlisting his colleagues' help at other universities, who in turn might ask their seminar students to take part in the project. Thus quite a lot depended upon cooperation between the principal university professors, but cooperation was not one of their distinguishing marks. They were rather thriving on debate and controversy which often bordered on open hostility and personal polemics. The Verein was also chronically hampered by lack of funds. More than one project was held up for financial reasons [17, p. 66].

Besides these organizational drawbacks there was the whole climate of values that the 'socialsts of the chair' had created, which prevailed both in the universities and the Verein. Debate and reform were the foremost concern. Survey technology was almost entirely neglected and did not become cumulative. Schumpeter who knew many of the most important economists and Verein members as a student and young professor, was quite outspoken in his criticism of the historical school of economics [129, p. 802]: 'The German 'socialists of the chair' certainly fulfilled the ideal of the professor who preaches reform and denounces obstructing interests. Lujo Brentano addressed his classes as he would political meetings, and they responded with cheers and countercheers. Adolph Wagner shouted and stamped and shook his fists at imaginary opponents, at least before the lethargy of old age quieted him down.' Perhaps not unrelated to this climate of values, the quality of economics was at a low level. A young economist might show a little ability in describing the trade practices among milk distributors, then be loud in voicing his approval of the ideals of the Verein and his reputation would be made, his future assured. Under such circumstances there was little incentive to create and to engage in the pedestrian tasks involved in social research. As Schumpeter put it [129, p. 804]: 'Otherwise excellent men ceased to care for the higher spheres of scientiflc invention and rigor.' Beyond the lack of imaginative innovation and interest in methodological issues which the overriding concern with social reform helped maintain, there was also the suspicion of the state authorities for an intellectual discipline which was so closely identified with 'leftist' political sympathies. Tönnies [151, p. 426] thought that it was in large part for this reason that sociology did not become officially recognized as an academic discipline, and in consequence no chair for it established in the universities before the war.

More difficult to assess than even the question of organization and value climate are such matters as the intellectual climate, the foci of interest and the formulation of problems in such a way that they are recognized as empirical problems. We have seen how the manner of conceptualizing public opinion as undifferentiated and inevitably molded by the press to its own designs   was probably preventing the empirical study of it, since the central problem of how people are influenced and how effectively that is done was prematurely answered in the formulation of the concept of public opinion itself. Michels' study of political parties focused on problems of leadership and organization. It could therefore be based on existing institutional records, newspaper reports and the accounts of the political leaders themselves. Had the question of participation by the rank and file appeared problematical to him and his contemporaries, they would have been forced into areas where there were not readily available data. The great question of the day for social scientists was, of course, the origin and spread of capitalism. Since this was an eminently historical problem, it could be answered without the aid of contemporary social research.

Lack of conceptual clarity was also a factor which prevented the empirical study of the family. At the time of Le Play, Quetelet and Engel there were excellent family budgets available and theoretically promising ideas about their significance. Yet as the years went by, the methodology of most budget studies deteriorated and they were carried out without any reference to Engels' budget law. All the descriptive and empirical work on living conditions, wages, migration, factory work, crime, etc., was not viewed from the more theoretical perspective of urbanization, family disorganization or deviant behavior. The intellectual tradition of broad theories of historical and economic development probably impeded the formulation of a more limited theoretical conceptualization which might have been brought to bear on the data available. In turn the lack of conceptual clarity failed to upgrade the fact-finding activities. Instead of progress along a course however dimly charted, there was but endless repetition of the same procedures with the same aims.

Another important development which set back the emergence of systematic social research was the division of labor between the social bookkeeping of administrative statistics and its analytical utilization by social scientists in the universities. Already in the heyday of moral statistics, Wagner and Conrad had called attention to the prohibitive task facing the lone scholar and his seminar students in their exploitation of the available statistical material. After the turn of the century when the relationship between statistics and sociology became a matter of discussion, the vacuum produced by this intellectual division of labor was noted again and again. In 1916 Ferdinand Schmid wrote that [118, p. 6] 'serious statisticians are looking with great concern on the growing 'cemetery of numbers' and the considerable overproduction of statistical data, and are demanding a further sociological penetration of the numerical mass observations.' It was no coincidence that the creation of social research or social statistical institutes was most frequently demanded by men like Tönnies who were engaged in an analytical treatment of social statistics.

Max Weber's efforts to establish an enduring tradition of empirical social research has so far never been documented. One reason is that they ended in failure, whereas his historical and theoretical works were such obvious successes. But Weber's frustrations in trying to break through the combination of colleague apathy, unfavorable value climate and lack of resources deserve to be spelled out in detail. The years 1910-1911 are the crucial moments in this drama. As a young professor Weber had had a taste of social research in the two surveys of peasants and agricultural laborers that he was involved in. Later

in his Heidelberg seminar he was still very much puzzled about how
to utilize survey data. With his mental breakdown he interrupted a
normal academic career until 1904 when his great period of intellectual achievements began. At that time Weber became extremely
interested in Levenstein's survey, and when Levenstein obstinately
refused to let university students and professors analyze the returns in
systematic fashion, Weber succeeded in pressuring him subtly into
doing it himself while at the same time offering advice on how it
ought to be done. The first great attitude survey thus was not lost
to science. In 1909 Weber became the unofficial head of the Verein
für Sozialpolitik survey of industrial workers for which he did most of
the conceptualization and study design while also engaging in extensive
computational work as preparation. At this time Weber also became
disenchanted with the Verein as an organization for sponsoring and
carrying out social surveys of scientific significance. In 1910 he was
active in founding the German Sociological Society whose primary
purpose was expressed in paragraph I of its constitution as 'the advancement of social science knowledge through the undertaking of scientific
investigations and surveys.' In his opening speech as treasurer of the
Society, Weber underlined that the Society be not conceived of as an
academy with an emphasis on honorific activities, but as an association
for large, collectively undertaken projects [166, p. 40]. He proceeded
to outline his ideas on the two first such projects, a survey of the press
and a survey of voluntary associations and organizations 'from the
bowling club – let us say it outright – to the political party and to the
religious, artistic or literary sect.' He busied himself immediately
with raising funds for these two vast projects. These activities deserve
to be documented for they reveal Weber's earnest efforts to establish
social research on a permanent basis.

In 1909 Weber had refused to join the newly founded Heidelberg
Academy of Sciences because its charter put too much emphasis on
historical research to the neglect of social research. 'How much more
fruitful it would be,' wrote Weber [150, p. 557],[1] 'if a modern academy
supported badly needed investigations that throw light on contemporary issues, rather than commit itself in favor of historical and

[1] Weber's plans for a social research institute were quoted in full by Tönnies in
an attempt to legitimize his own efforts in getting 'sociographic observatories'
established in the post-war period. Tönnies managed to obtain Weber's unpublished
notes on these matters from Marianne Weber.

philosophical studies which a single individual can perfrom so easily
by himself anyway.' Weber eventually did manage to make his
membership contingent upon financial support of the Academy of
his newspaper survey to the extent of 2,000 Marks a year for five years,
yet he lost out on his broader plan of getting a research institute started. 'The creation of the Academy has not the slightest value for the
systematic disciplines as opposed to the others (Weber means by this
always the historical disciplines).[2] Something will only be accomplished if the academy were first of all willing to support *continuously*
and with large sums great collective undertakings, especially the
surveys themselves and in the economic disciplines also the numerical
computations based on the survey material or on the figures already
assembled in official statistical publications; and secondly, if the
academy provided *systematically* sums of money earmarked to promising
young men, after the completion of their formal schooling, for voyages
abroad, in order to make systematic inquiries under the direct supervision of the active representatives of their discipline. For the actual
functioning of legal institutions and the constitution, as well as the
social foundations upon which the political, economic, and cultural
development of nations rests, could be studied fruitfully only in this
manner' [151, p. 430]. From this draft of Weber it would appear that
he had no less than a social research institute in mind, complete with
computational facilities, and a postgraduate system of fellowships for
foreing travel and area studies. This is, after all, not very different
from the institutional support which makes systematic research possible
today in the United States.

The survey of the press never went beyond the planning stage.
Weber got himself involved in the so-called N. N. affair [158, pp.
434-445] which started when an anonymous newspaper article
attacked his wife's role in the women's emancipation movement in
insulting language. Subsequently there were even hints made that
Weber had refused to fight a duel in defense of his wife's honor which
infuriated him no end. The whole unpleasant matter came to a head
in a court trial during which the principle of anonymity would became
a major issue. Weber felt rightly that these activities would jeopardize
the cooperation of editors and other influential figures in the newspaper
world, should he remain the head of the survey. Weber did not

---

[2] The parentheses are an explanatory note by Tönnies inserted into the Weber
text he quoted from.

however find a suitable substitute. There was generally lack of interest among the other members of the German Sociological Society for collective research undertakings. Marianne Weber reported these events in no uncertain terms [158, p. 429]: 'It became especially evident that none of the 'great ones' were willing to lead the collective investigations. The organization of the newspaper survey remained stuck on Weber. For months he makes a great effort to get the work going but he is left to seek help among real beginners. A few valuable investigations are finally produced, but because of the difficult nature of the subject matter, only on partial aspects of the problem. The same fate falls upon the survey of associations. After a year and a half of efforts Weber realizes that he is merely wasting his energies.' Although it is impossible to know what went on behind the scenes at the German Sociological Society, it is certain that Weber handed in his resignation as treasurer already at the second meeting in 1912 when he realized that he was getting nowhere with his collective empirical undertakings. The World War followed shortly thereafter, and with it Weber was drawn for a time into the administration of a hospital for wounded soldiers. Later on he devoted his full energies to political activity on behalf of his country. He died too soon after the war to pursue his fight for social research.

Weber and Tönnies were not the only figures who at this time perceived the need for a social research institute to be established outside of the academic structure. In 1911 three Berlin law professors sent out a circular concerning the creation of a German Institute for Legal Philosophy and Sociological Research to about 25 prominent jurists and other professors both in Germany and abroad [74].[3] All

---

[3] The relationship between law and sociology has not been adequately dealt with in the literature on the history of sociology. Further research on this matter would undoubtedly shed some new light on the rise of social theory at the turn of the century. Law professors sometimes engaged directly in social research. In 1906 Martin Wolff [176], law professor in Berlin, published a questionnaire in a legal journal to be answered by public notaries and judges on the relationship between legal norms as they are set down in the statute books and the actual behavior and customs of the people. Wolff saw the need to transcend the limited range of experience of single individuals (p. 697): 'A true picture of the customs of the German people can only be gotten if the testimony of many practicing professionals from all parts of Germany is available and exploited methodically.' Wolff justified his excursion into a novel field by noting that (p. 698) 'the political economists were hardly ever concerned with the questions here raised.' Two years later another lawyer, Martin Segall, published the results of the survey in a legal journal [130].

but one reply came out in favor of such an institute, although it is evident that most of the law professors had in mind an institute of comparative law rather than the Weberian type of social research institute. Georg von Mayr, Tönnies and Leopold von Wiese were among the professors queried, and all three came out strongly for the idea, though they were pessimistic about the prospects for positive action. Von Wiese especially (pp. 223-224) thought that the notion that the cultural sciences needed laboratories to conduct inductive and experimental investigations like the natural sciences was so counter to prevailing opinion that it did not have much of a chance of being accepted. The dissenting opinion came from the noted historian and publicist Hans Delbrück who denied the existence and even the possibility of sociology as a distinct discipline with a distinct method of procedure (pp. 208-209). Delbrück was probably representative of a large body of opinion among historians who looked upon the emergence of sociology with considerable hostility. Another example was the lifelong opposition of the economic historian Georg von Below to sociology. In his polemical writings he tried to associate sociology with positivism, naturalism, socialism, and other 'foreign influences' both harmful and unnecessary for the development of German science [8]. It would seem therefore that among the unfavorable factors for the emergence of sociology and social research the hostility of neighboring disciplines within the university walls has also to be included. At any rate the Institute for Legal Philosophy and Sociological Research, like similar plans for the establishment of research institutes in sociology, did not come into being.

Eugen Ehrlich [38], another law professor, for many years advocated that psychology, sociology and economics be taught to law students. He himself conducted a 'seminar on living law' at the University of Czernowitz. He took field trips with the students into nearby factories and villages. Because of financial limitations his aims were primarily pedagogic, but he hoped to secure support for full scale 'legal surveys' of entire villages, factories, and communities in the course of which all titles, property rights, contractual relationships, and actual practices would be carefully recorded.

Bibliography

Abbrevations

Allgemeiner Statisticher Archiv – *All. Stat. Ar.*
Archiv für Sozialwissenschaft und Sozialpolitik – *Archiv.*
Handwörterbuch der Staatswissenschaften – *H. w. B. Staats.*
Jahrbuch für Gesetzgebung, Verwaltung und Volkswirtschaft im Deutchen
Reich – *Schmollers Jb.*
Jahrbücher für Nationaloekonomie und Statistik – *Jb. f. Nat. u Stat..*
Münchner Volkswirtschaftliche Studien – *Munch. Volk. St.*
Schriften des Vereins für Sozialpolitik – *Verein.*
Staats- und Sozialwissenschaftliche Forschungen — *Staats. u. Soz. For.*
Zeitschrift für die gesammte Staatswissenschaft – *Z. f. d. g. Staats.*

1. Abbe, Ernst, *Gesammelte Schriften III* (Jena: Gustav Fischer, 1906).
2. Ackerknecht, Erwin, *Rudolf Virchow, Doctor, Statesman, Anthropologist* (Madison: U. of Wisconsin Press, 1953).
3. Allgemeine Konferenz der Deutschen Sittlichkeitsvereine, *Die geschlechtlichsittliche Verhältnisse der evangelitschen Landbewohnern* (Leipzig, 1895).
4. Altenloh, Emilie, *Zur Soziologie des Kino* (Jena: Diederichs, 1914).
5. Ammon, Otto, *Die Gesellschaftsordnung und ihre natürliche Grundlagen* (Jena: Gustav Fischer, 1895).
6. Asher, 'Die ländliche Arbeiterwohnungen in Preussen,' in *Schriften der Centralstelle für Arbeiterwohlfahrtseinrichtungen 13* (1897).
7. Baritz, Loren, *The Servants of Power* (Middletown: Wesleyan U. P., 1960).
8. Below, Georg von, 'Soziologie als Lehrfach,' in *Schmollers Jb. 43* (1919), 1271-1325.
9. Bendix, Reinhard, *Max Weber* (Garden City, N. Y: Doubleday, 1960).
10. Bernays, Marie, 'Gladbacher Spinnerei und Weberei,' in *Verein 133* (1910).
11. Bernays, Marie, 'Psychophysik der Textilarbeit,' in *Archiv 32* (1911), 99-123.
12. ——,Book review of [88] in *Archiv 35* (1912), 832-833.
13. Bernsdorf, W. and Gottfried Eiserman, *Die Einheit der Sozialwissenschaften* (Stuttgart: Emke, 1938).
14. Bernhard, Ernst, 'Höhere Arbeitsintensität bei kürzerer Arbeitzeit,' in *Staats. u. Soz. For. Heft 138* (1909).

15. Blank, R., 'Die soziale Zusammensetzung der sozialdemokratischen Wählerschaft Deutschlands,' in *Archiv 20* (1904/05), 507-553.
16. Bleibtreu, Carl, *Das Heer* (Frankfurt a.M.: Rütten und Loenig, 1910).
17. Boese, Franz, *Geschichte des Vereins für Sozialpolitik* (Berlin: Duncker u. Humblot, 1939).
18. Borell, Adolf, *Die soziologische Gliederung des Reichsparlaments* (Dissertation, Giessen, 1933).
19. v. Bortkievitz, Ludwig, 'Die Mittlere Lebensdauer,' in *Staatswissenschaftliche Studien 4, Heft 6* (1909).
20. Bottomore, T. B. and M. Rubel, eds., *Karl Marx, Selected Writings in Sociology and Social Philosophy* (London: Wells, 1956).
21. Braun, Adolf, 'Die Reichstagwahlen von 1898 und 1903,' in *Archiv 18* (1903), 539-563.
22. Brentano Lujo, 'Uber einige in der Natur des Beobachtungsobjekts liegende Schwierigkeiten des Volkswirtschaftlichen Forschens,' in *Archiv 38* (1914), 58-82.
23. ——,*Mein Leben* (Jena: Diederichs, 1931).
24. ——,'Dr. Gottlieb Schnapper-Arndt,' in *Süddeutsche Monatshefte 3-II* (1906), 207-210.
25. Bromme, Moritz W., *Lebensgeschichte eines modernen Fabrikarbeiters* (Jena: 1905).
26. Bücher, Karl, 'Haushaltungsbudgets oder Wirtschaftsrechnungen,' in *Z. f. d. g. Staats. 62* (1906), 686-700.
27. ——,*Arbeit und Rhytmus*, 2nd ed. (Leipzig: 1899).
28. ——, *Gesammelte Aufsätze zur Zeitungskunde* (Tübingen: Laupp, 1926).
29. Conrad, Johannes, 'Beitrag zur Untersuchung des Einflusses von Lebensstellung und Beruf auf die Moralitätsverhältnisse,' in *Sammlung nationalökonomischer und statistischer Abhandlungen zu Halle*, Vol. I, #2 (1877).
30. ——, 'Das Universitätsstudium in Deutschland während der letzten 50 Jahre,' in *Sammlung nationalökonomischer und statistischer Abhandlungen zu Halle*, Vol. III, #2 (1884).
31. Czuber, Ernst, 'Die Entwicklung der Wahrscheinlichkeitstheorie und ihre Anwendung,' in *Jahresbericht der Deutschen Mathematiker-Vereinigung 7, Heft 2* (1889).
32. Dehn, Günther, *Proletarische Jugend* (Berlin: Furcheverlag, 1923).
33. Demeter, Karl, *Das Deutsche Heer und seine Offiziere* (Berlin: Hobbing, 1935).
34. Drobisch, Moritz W., *Die Moralische Statistik und die Menschliche Willensfreiheit* (Leipzig: Voss, 1867).
35. Eger, Hans, *Der Evangelisch-Soziale Kongress* (Leipzig: Heinsius, 1931).
36. Ehrenberg, Richard and Hugo Racine,' Kruppsche Arbeiterfamilien.' in *Archiv für Exakte Wirtschaftsforschung, Ergänzungsheft 6* (1912).
37. Ehrenberg, Richard, 'Plan zur Einrichtung eines Instituts für exakte Wirtschaftsforschung,' in *Thünen Archiv 2* (1909), 167-175, 311-315.
38. Ehrlich, Eugen, 'Ausbildung der Juristen,' in *Verhandlungen des 31 Deutschen Juristentages. Gutachten II* (1912), 200-220.

39. Embden, G., 'Wie sind Enqueten zu organisieren.' in *Verein 13* (1877), 1-15.

40. Engel, Ernst, 'Die Produktions und Consumtionsverhältnisse des Königreichs Sachsen,' in *Zeitschrift des Stat. Bür. des Konigl. Säch. Minist. des Inneren Nos. 8&9* (Nov. 22, 1857).

41. ——, *Die Lebenskosten Belgischer Arbeiterfamilien* (Dresden: Heinrich, 1895).

42. Engels, Friedrich, *Die Lage der Arbeitenden Klassen in England*, 2nd ed. (Stuttgart: Dietz, 1892).

43. Erdmann, August, *Die Christliche Arbeiterbewegung in Deutschland* (Stuttgart: Dietz, 1909).

44. Eulenberg, Franz, 'Die Frequenz der Deutschen Universitäten von ihrer Gründung bis zur Gegenwart,' in *Abhandlungen der philologisch-historischen Klasse der königl. sächs. Gesellschaft der Wissenschaft 24* (1904), #2.

45. ——, 'Das Alter der Deutschen Universitätsprofessoren,' in *Jb. Nat. u. Stat. 80* (1903), 65-80.

46. ——, 'Der Akademische Nachwuchs,' in *Archiv 27* (1908), 808-825.

47. Fick, Ludwig, 'Die Bäuerliche Erbsfolge im Rechtsrheinischen Bayern', in *Munch. Volk. Stud. Heft 8* (1895).

48. Fischer, Karl, *Denkwürdigkeiten und Erinnergungen eines Arbeiters* (Leipzig: 1904).

49. Fromont, Louis, *Une Expérience Industrielle de la Réduction de la Journée de Travail* (Bruxelles: Misch & Thron, 1906).

50. Gerson, Adolf, 'Die physiologischen Grundlagen der Arbeitsteilung,' in *Zeitschrift für Sozialwissenschaft 10* (1907).

51. Gewerkschaftsbund der Angestellten, *Die Wirtschaftliche und Soziale Lage der Angestellten* (Berlin: Sieben-Stäbe, 1931).

52. Göhre, Paul, *Drei Monate Fabrikarbeiter* (Leipzig: Grunow, 1891).

53. Goldschmidt, Sally, *Die Landarbeiter in der Provinz Sachsen* (Thesis, Heidelberg, 1899).

54. Goltz, Theodor v. d., *Die Lage der ländlichen Arbeiter im Deutschen Reich* (Berlin: 1875).

55. Grotjahn, Alfred, *Soziale Pathologie* (1915).

56. ——, and F. Kriegel, *Jahresbericht über soziale Hygiene, Demographie, und Sozialstatistik 1902-1915*.

57. Hellpach, Willy, Book review of [88] in *Archiv 36* (1913), 929-938.

58. ——, *Gruppenfabrikation* (Berlin: Springer, 1922).

59. ——, *Einleitung in die Völkerpsychologie* (Stuttgart: Emke, 1938).

60. Herkner, Heinrich, 'Die Oberelsässische Baumwollindustrie und ihre Arbeiter,' in *Verhandlungen aus dem Staatswissenschaftlichen Seminar zu Strassburg 4* (1887).

61. ——, *Die Arbeiterfrage*, 8th ed. (Leipzig: de Gruyler, 1922).

62. ——, Book review of [88] in *Jb. f. Nat. u Stat. 99* (1913), 698-702.

63. Heuss, Theodor, *Friedrich Naumann* (Stuttgart: Deutsche Verlag, 1937).

64. Heyde, Ludwig, 'Die Trinkgeldablösung im Gastgewerbe,' in *Schriften der Gesellschaft für Sozialreform 6, Heft 1* (1901).

65. Hildebrand, Bruno, 'Die Wissenschaftliche Aufgabe der Statistik,' in *Jb. f. Nat. u. Stat. 6* (1866) *1-11*.

66. Hirschberg, E,. *Die Sociale Lage der Arbeitenden Klassen in Berlin* (Berlin: 1897).

67. Hofmann, Walter, 'Zur Psychologie des Proletariats,' in *Volksbildungsarchiv 1* (1910), 227-344.

68. Horkheimer, Max, ed., *Studien über Autorität und Familie* (Paris: Felix Alcan, 1936).

69. Hughes, H. Stuart, *Consciousness and Society* (New York: Knopf, 1958).

70. Ilgenstein, W., *Die religiöse Gedankenwelt der Sozialdemokratie* (Berlin: 1914).

71. Jacoby, E. G., 'Ferdinand Tönnies, Sociologist,' in *Kyklos* (1955), 144-157.

72. John, Viktor, *Geschichte der Statistik* (Stuttgart: Emke, 1894).

73. Kaufmann, Felix, *Methodenlehre der Sozialwissenschaften* (Wien: Springer, 1936).

74. Klose, Olaf, E. G. Jacoby and Irma Fischer, eds., *Ferdinand Tönnies-Friedrich Paulsen: Briefwechsel, 1876-1908* (Kiel: Hirt, 1961).

75. Knapp, G. F., *Über die Ermittelung der Sterblichkeit aus den Aufzeichnungen der Bevölkerungsstatistik* (Leipzig: 1868).

76. Knies, Karl, *Die Statistik als Selbstständige Wissenschaft* (Kassel: 1850).

77. Koch, Adalbert, 'Arbeitermemoiren als Sozialwissenschaftliche Erkenntnisquelle,' in *Archiv 61* (1929), 128-167.

78. Kohler, J., von Liszt, F., and F. Beroltzheimer, 'Ein Deutsches Institut für Rechtsphilosophie und Soziologische Forschung?' in *Archiv für Rechts- und Wirtschaftsphilosophie 4* (1910/11), 190-225.

79. Kracauer, Siegfried, *Die Angestellten* (Frankfurt: 1930).

80. Kremer, Willy, *Der Soziale Aufbau der Partein des Deutschen Reichstages von 1871-1918* (Dissertation, Köhn, 1934).

81. Lazarsfeld, P. F., and M. Rosenberg, eds., *The Language of Social Research* (Glencoe: The Free Press, 1955).

82. Lazarsfeld, Paul F., 'Notes on the History of Quantification in Sociology,' in *Isis 52, Part 2* (June 1961), 277-333.

83. Leipart, Theodor, ed., *Die Lage der Arbeiter in der Holzindustrie* (Stuttgart: 1902).

84. ——, *Arbeitszeit und Löhne in der Holzindustrie* (Stuttgart: 1908).

85. Lengerke v., Alexander, *Die Ländliche Arbeiterfrage* (Berlin: 1849).

86. Levenstein, Adolf, *Aus der Tiefe* (Berlin: Morgenverlag, 1909).

87. ——, *Arbeiterphilosophen und Dichter* (Berlin: Morgenverlag, 1909).

88. ——, *Die Arbeiterfrage* (München: Rheinhardt, 1912).

89. Lexis, Wilhelm, *Zur Theorie der Massenerscheinungen* (Freiburg: 1877).

90. ——, ed., *Das Unterrichtswesen im Deutschen Reich* (Berlin: Asher, 1904).

91. Löbl, Emil, *Kultur und Presse* (Leipzig: Duncker & Hublot, 1903).

92. Lowie, R., *The German People* (New York: Rinehart and Co., 1945).

93. Maas, Fritz, 'Über die Herkunftsbedingungen der geistigen Führer,' in *Archiv 41* (1915/16), 144-186.

94. Mannhardt, Wilhelm, *Roggenwolf und Roggenhund* (Danzig: 1865).

95. Matte, Wilhelm, 'Die Bayrischen Bauernräte,' in *Munch. Volk. St.* *144* (1921).
96. May, Eugen, *Mein Lebenslauf* (Berlin: Springer, 1922).
97. May, Max, *Wie der Arbeiter Lebt* (Berlin: Heymans, 1896).
98. Mayr v., Georg, *Statistik und Gesellschaftslehre I-III* (Freiburg: Mohr, 1895-1917).
99. Michels, Robert, 'Psychologie der Antikapitalistischen Bewegung,' in *Grundriss der Sozialökonomik IX, part I* (Tübingen: Mohr, 1926).
100. Mosse, M. and G. Tugendrich, eds., *Krankheit und Soziale Lage* (1913).
101. Most, Otto, 'Zur Wirtschafts-und Sozialstatistik der höheren Beamten in Preussen,' in *Schmollers Jb. 39* (1915), 181-218.
102. Münsterberg, Hugo, *Psychology and Industrial Efficiency* (Boston: Mifflin, 1913).
103. Münsterberg, Hugo, *Grundzüge der Psychotechnik* (Leipzig: Barth, 1914).
104. Niceforo, Alfredo, *Les Classes Pauvres* (Paris: 1905).
105. Noussance, Henry de, 'Que vaut la presse quotidienne francaise?' in *Revue Hebdomadaire* (June 1902), 1-26.
106. Piechowski, Paul, *Proletarischer Glaube* (Berlin: Furche, 1927).
107. Ploetz, Alfred, 'Sozialpolitik und Rassenbiologie,' in *Archiv 17* (1902), 393-420.
108. ——, 'Die Begriffe Rasse und Gesellschaft,' in *Schriften der Deutschen Gesellschaft für Soziologie 1* (1911), 111-165.
109. Popp, Adelhaide, *The Autobiography of a Working Woman* (London: Unwin, 1912).
110. Rade, Max, 'Die religiöse-sittliche Gedankenwelt unserer Industrie-arbeiter,' in *Verhandlungen des Neunten Evangelisch-Sozialen Kongresses, 1898.*
111. Reichskanzleramt, *Ergebnisse der über die Verhältnisse der Lehrling, Gesellen und Fabrikarbeiter angestellten Erhebungen* (Berlin: 1877).
112. Riehl, Wilhem H., *Die Naturgeschichte des Volkes I-IV* (Stuttgart: Cotta, 1856).
113. ——, *Die Volkskunde als Wissenschaft* (Berlin: Stubenruch, 1935).
114. Rigaudias-Weiss, Hilde, *Les Enquêtes Ouvrières en France entre 1830 et 1848* (Paris: P. U. F., 1936).
115. Rosen, George, *A History of Public Health* (New York: MD Publications, 1958).
116. ——, 'What is Social Medicine', in *Bulletin of Medical History 21* (1947) 674-733.
117. Schacht, Hjalmar, 'Statistische Untersuchung über die Presse Deutschlands,' in *Jb. f. Nat. u. Stat. 70* (1898), 503-525.
118. Schmid, Ferdinand, 'Statistik und Soziologie,' in *All. Stat. Ar. 10* (1916), 1-74.
119. Schmoller, Gustav, 'Die neueren Ansichten über Bevölkerungs-und Moralstatistik,' in *Zur Literaturgeschichte der Staats-und Sozialwissenschaften* (Leipzig: Duncker und Humblot, 1888), 172-203.
120. ——, 'Die Volkswirtschaft und ihre Methode,' in *H. w. B. Staats. 6* (1894), 527-562.

121. Schnabel, Franz, *Deutsche Geschichte im XIX Jahrhundert* (Freiburg: Herder, 1954).
122. Schnapper-Arndt, Gottlieb, 'Fünf dorfgemeinden auf dem Hohen Taunus,' in *Staats. u. Soz. For. 16* (1883).
123. ——, *Methodologie Sozialer Enqueten* (Frankfurt a.M.: 1888).
124. ——, *Vorträge und Aufsätze I-III* (Tübingen: 1906).
125. ——, *Sozialstatistik* (Leipzig: Klinkhardt, 1908).
126. Schönberg, Gustav, *Arbeitsämter, eine Aufgabe des Deutschen Reiches* (Berlin: 1871).
127. Schöne, 'Die Statistik als Grundlage der empirischen Soziologie,' in *Jb. Nat. u. Stat. III* (1918), 257-290.
128. Schumacher, Hermann, 'Staatswissenschaften,' in Gustav Abb, ed., *50 Jahren Deutscher Wissenschaften* (Berlin: Gruyter, 1930), 136-150.
129. Schumpeter, Joseph, *History of Economic Analysis* (New York: Oxford U. P., 1954).
130. Segall, Martin, 'Das bürgerliche Recht und die Lebensgewohnheiten,' in *Archiv für bürgerliches Recht 32* (1908), 410-457.
131. Spann, Othmar, 'Die Verpflegungsverhältnisse der unehelichen Kinder,' in *Archiv 27* (1908), 686-729.
132. Steinhausen, Georg, *Deutsche Geistes und Kulturgeschichte von 1870 bis zur Gegenwart* (Halle: Niemeyer, 1931).
133. Steinmetz, S. R., 'Der Nachwuchs der Begabten,' in *Zeitschrift für Sozialwissenschaft I* (1904), 1-25.
134. Stoklossa, Paul, 'Der Inhalt der Zeitungen,' in *Z. f. d. g. Staats. 66* (1910), 555-565.
135. Thun, Alphons, 'Die Industrie am Niederrhein und ihre Arbeiter,' in *Staats. u. Soz. For. II, Heft 2 & 3* (1879).
136. Tönnies, Ferdinand, 'Kriminal-Anthropologie,' in *Zeitschrift für Psychologie und Physiologie der Sinnesorgane 2* (1891), 321-334.
137. ——, 'Das Verbrechen als Soziale Erscheinung,' in *Archiv 8* (1895), 329-344.
138. ——, 'Der Hamburger Streik von 1896/7,' in *Archiv 10* (1897), 173-238, 673-720.
139. ——, 'Die Ostseehafen Flensburg, Kiel, Lübeck,' in *Verein 104* (1903), 512-614.
140. ——, 'Die Anwendung der Deszendenztheorie auf Probleme der sozialen Entwicklung,' in *Soziologischen Studien und Kritiken III* (Jena: Fischer, 1929), 133-329.
141. ——, 'Eine Neue Methode zur Vergleichung Statistischer Reihen,' in *Schmollers Jb. 33* (1909), 699-720.
142. ——, 'Agrarstatistik,' in *Archiv 30* (1910), 285-332.
143. ——, 'Die Gesetzmässigkeit in der Bewegung der Bevölkerung,' in *Archiv 39* (1915), 150-173, 767-794.
144. ——, 'Verbrechertum in Schleswig-Holstein I,' in *Archiv 52* (1924), 761-797.
145. ——, 'Das Verbrechertum in Schleswig-Holstein II,' in *Archiv 58* (1927), 608-628.

146. ——, 'Das Verbrechertum in Schleswig-Holstein III,' in *Archiv 61* (1929), 322-359.

147. ——, 'Korrelation der Parteien in der Statistik der Kieler Reichtags-wahlen,' in *Jb. f. Nat. u. Stat. 122* (1924), 663-672.

148. ——, *Soziologische Studien und Kritiken III* (Jena: Fischer, 1929).

149. ——, 'Der Selbstmord in Schleswig-Holstein,' in *Veröffentlichungen der Schleswig-Holsteinschen Universitätsgesellschaft 9* (1927).

150. ——, 'Statistik und Soziographie,' in *All. Stat. Ar. 18* (1928), 546-561.

151. ——, 'Sozialwissenschaftliche Forschungsinstitute,' in Brauer L., A. Mendelssohn and A. Meyer, eds., *Forschungsinstitute I* (Hamburg: Haltung, 1930), 425-440.

152. Verein für Sozialpolitik, *Schriften*, 188 vols. (Berlin: Duncker u. Humblot, 1872-1939).

153. Virchow, Rudolf, 'Mitteilungen über die in Oberschlesien herschende Typhus-Epidemie,' in *Öffentliche Medizin I* (Berlin: Hirschwald, 1879).

154. Vogel, Walter, *Bismarcks Arbeiterversicherung* (Braunschweig: Westermann, 1951).

155. Vorstand des Deutschen Metallarbeiterverbandes, *Die Schwerindustrie* (Stuttgart: 1912).

156. Wagner, Adolph, *Die Gesetzmässigkeit in den Scheinbar Willkürlichen Menschlichen Handlungen vom Standpunkte der Statistik* (Hamburg: Geisler, 1864).

157. Weber, Alfred, 'Das Berufsschicksal der Industriearbeiter,' in *Archiv 34* (1912), 377-405.

158. Weber, Marianne, *Max Weber, Ein Lebensbild* (Tübingen: Mohr, 1926).

159. Weber, Max, 'Die Verhältnisse der Landarbeiter im Ostelbischen Deutschland,' in *Verein 55* (1892).

160. ——, 'Die Erhebungen des Evangelisch-Sozialen Kongresses über die Verhältnisse der Landarbeiter Deutschlands,' in *Christliche Welt* (1893), 535-540.

161. ——, *The Protestant Ethic and the Spirit of Capitalism* (New York: Scribner, 1958).

162. ——, 'National Character and the Junkers,' in Gerth, Hans, and C. W. Mills, eds., *From Max Weber* (New York: Oxford U.P., 1958), 386-395.

163. ——, 'Erhebungen über Anpassung und Auslese (Berufswahl und Berufsschicksal) der Arbeiterschaft der geschlossenen Gross-industrie,' in *Gesammelte Aufsätze zur Soziologie und Sozialpolitik* (Tübingen: Mohr, 1924), 1-60.

164. ——, 'Zur Psychophysik der industriellen Arbeit,' in *Gesammelte Aufsätze zur Soziologie und Sozialpolitik* (Tübingen: Mohr, 1924), 61-225.

165. ——, 'Zur Methodik Sozialpsychologischer Enqueten und ihrer Bearbeitung,' in *Archiv 29* (1909), 949-958.

166. ——, 'Geschäftbericht der Deutschen Gesellschaft für Soziologie,' in *Schriften der Deutschen Gesellschaft für Soziologie I* (1911), 39-62.

167. ——, 'The Socialpsychology of World Religions,' in Gerth, Hans, and C. W. Mills, eds., *From Max Weber* (New York: Oxford U.P., 1958), 386-395.

168. ——, 'Kategorien der Verstehenden Soziologie,' in *Soziologie, Weltgeschichtliche Analysen, Politik* (Stuttgart: Kröner, 1956), 97-150.

169. ——, 'Science as a Vocation,' in Gerth, Hans, and C. W. Mills, eds., *Essays from Max Weber* (New York: Oxford U.P., 1958), 129-156.

170. Weber, Max, ed., *Die Landarbeiter Deutschlands* (Tübingen: 1899).

171. Wettstein-Adelt, Minna, *3-1/2 Monate Fabrikarbeiterin* (Berlin: 1893).

172. Wiese, Leopold von, Book review of 'Die Arbeitslosen von Marienthal,' in *Kölner Vierteljahrshefte für Soziologie 12* (1934), 96-98.

173. Williams, Whiting, *What's on the Worker's Mind* (New York: Scribner, 1920).

174. Wittwer, M., *Das Deutsche Zeitungswesen in seiner Neueren Entwicklung* (Halle-Wittenberg: Dissertation, 1914).

175. Woerishoffer, Friedrich, *Die Soziale Lage der Fabrikarbeiter in Mannheim* (Karlsruhe: 1891).

176. Wolff, Martin, 'Das bürgerliche Gesetzbuch und die deutschen Lebensgewohnheiten,' in *Juristische Wochenschrift 35* (1906), 697-700.

177. Wuttke, Heinrich, *Die Deutschen Zeitungen und die Entstehung der Öffentlichen Meinung* (Leipzig: Krüger, 1875).

178. Ziegler, Henrich, *Einleitung zu dem Sammelwerk Natur und Staat* (Jena: Fischer, 1903).

179. Ziermer, Manfred, 'Genealogische Studien über die Vererbung geistigen Eigenschaften,' in *Archiv für Rassen- und Gesellschaftsbiologie 5* (1908), 178-220, 327-363.

180. Zizek, Franz, *Soziologie und Statistik* (Leipzig: Duncker u. Humblot, 1912).